Flora Haines Loughead

The abandoned Claim

Flora Haines Loughead

The abandoned Claim

ISBN/EAN: 9783743341678

Manufactured in Europe, USA, Canada, Australia, Japa

Cover: Foto ©ninafisch / pixelio.de

Manufactured and distributed by brebook publishing software (www.brebook.com)

Flora Haines Loughead

The abandoned Claim

THE ABANDONED CLAIM

BY

FLORA HAINES LOUGHEAD
AUTHOR OF "THE MAN WHO WAS GUILTY"

BOSTON AND NEW YORK
HOUGHTON, MIFFLIN AND COMPANY
The Riverside Press, Cambridge
1891

CONTENTS.

Chapter		Page
I.	The Shadow of Doom	1
II.	Ways and Means	7
III.	The Abandoned Claim	15
IV.	The Head of a Family	27
V.	Tom's Apology	33
VI.	The Man with a History	40
VII.	Crossing the Rubicon	49
VIII.	Discovery	56
IX.	A Tour of Exploration	61
X.	A Busy Day	71
XI.	A Home and Three Patriots	80
XII.	A Mysterious Journey	86
XIII.	Winter on a California Ranch	91
XIV.	The Rope Express	97
XV.	Hope and the Birds	106
XVI.	The Old Orchard	110
XVII.	Making Improvements	114
XVIII.	Two Surprises	120
XIX.	A Trip to the City	129
XX.	Hope's Embezzlement	133
XXI.	Hope's Indictment	139
XXII.	Hard Times	148
XXIII.	The Second Season	158
XXIV.	A Project and an Adventure	168
XXV.	A Premature Blast	176
XXVI.	The Building of the Bridge	186
XXVII.	A Prisoner of War	196
XXVIII.	How Hank Jones's Claim was Settled	208
XXIX.	How God Remembered	219
XXX.	Progress	226
XXXI.	How Tom kept His Word	233

XXXII.	A Newspaper Item	240
XXXIII.	The Prodigal Son	247
XXXIV.	Hope's Experiment	253
XXXV.	Hope's Black Rose and What came of It	258
XXXVI.	Martin tries to save Dr. John	266
XXXVII.	Dr. John is brought to Bay	272
XXXVIII.	At the Camp Fire	277
XXXIX.	Trouble in the Valley	284
XL.	The Court of Last Resort	293
XLI.	The Doctor's Story	299
XLII.	The Last Battle	305
XLIII.	The Miracle a Blunder wrought	320
XLIV.	Proving Up	323

THE ABANDONED CLAIM.

CHAPTER I.

THE SHADOW OF DOOM.

"How long has he been this way?"

It was a physician who spoke, a gray-bearded, elderly man, with a gruff, professional air, and kind blue eyes that belied his manner.

"He was taken down about three quarters of an hour ago. But, if you'll excuse me, sir, I think it's been coming on for some time. He's been queer and shaky-like for weeks. Started in to work this morning, and dropped down all in a heap, as you see him."

The rays of the morning sun entered the tall windows of the furniture factory, and filtered through the dust-laden air until they reached the corner where the speakers were standing. All work was suspended, and the frank faces of the workmen wore a common expression of honest concern over the calamity that had overtaken one of their number.

At the feet of the speakers, a man of unusual stature and herculean frame lay stretched upon a pile of shavings over which some sacking had been thrown. Body, limbs, muscles, even the features of his face, might have been fixed in an invisible frame of iron, so rigid and motionless were they. Only the brown eyes, large and gentle, looked forth with a piteous expression, telling that a sensitive human soul was still imprisoned in the helpless body.

"Never saw such a worker in my life," continued the first speaker, who was the foreman of the shop. "He could do the work of two men, and what is more, he was always trying to do it. No use holding him back! He was like some blooded horse, — always straining at the bit."

"Poor fellow. He's done his last day's work," said the doctor gravely.

"Burst a blood vessel? Dying? I thought so."

"Worse than that. Paralysis."

"My God! And he may live on, like that?"

"He may live for months. Probably another stroke will soon follow. That will be the end."

The doctor moved uneasily as he gave this verdict. Something in the man's face, something in the foreman's statement, invested the case with more than ordinary interest.

"Has the man any means, any one to take care of him? He ought not to lie here. The City and County Hospital cares for such cases" —

The foreman cut him short, with a decisive gesture.

"Very few hard-working, forehanded mechanics

ever come to that. I happen to know he is a paying member of the —— Mutual Benevolent Society. Most of our men belong to some association of that sort. Danger of accident, you know. That has its own hospital, and will take care of him as long as he lives. It's bound to."

"Better send for the ambulance at once, then."

The foreman stepped to the telephone, shouted to the main office, waited a moment, and shouted again.

The physician turned to go. Other calls were pressing, other patients waiting. There was plainly no money in this case: yet one more question forced itself upon him: —

"Has he any family?"

The foreman's face clouded with unpleasant recollection.

"The wife died last year," he explained in a low voice. "There are three children. He set a store by them. We sent for them. There they are now."

There they stood, on the threshold of the great shop, and, unconsciously, on the threshold of a new life. Three children, two boys and a girl, with their school satchels on their arms, and a look of anxiety and dread overcasting their youthful faces.

The boys were the oldest, fine, manly fellows of twelve and fifteen years, the elder with something of his father's noble physique. The girl was a year or two younger, a quiet, inconspicuous little creature, who shrank back at the sight of the large room and the strange men there; yet she was the first to go forward as their eyes swept the place and fell on the prostrate figure at the further end. Quietly and swiftly, like one accustomed to duties of the sick-room, she sped to her father's side and knelt by his pallet, chafing his rough hands between her own. The boys followed, and helplessly looked down upon him.

"What is the matter?"

Her white lips seemed to shape the words. The physician, lingering against his will, answered shortly: —

"Paralysis. He must go to the hospital. The ambulance is coming for him."

"Why not home? We can take care of him. He will get well sooner there."

It was Ned, the eldest, who spoke. The doctor turned away. The boy touched his arm, repeating the question. There was no answer. He appealed to the foreman.

"Mr. Graves, you don't think — He does n't mean — that father won't get well?"

Then the blow fell upon them, and fell heavily, and all the men within hearing turned away, unable to bear the sight.

Somebody announced that the ambulance had come, but no one seemed willing to disturb the little girl, who still hung over the sick man, kissing his forehead, smoothing his hair with her hand, whispering endearing words, choking back her own grief and pain, to comfort him, with womanly tenderness.

The lips of the stricken man moved, but only an inarticulate murmur escaped.

"He is trying to say something," declared the foreman.

The girl listened intently. The physician bent down his head.

"'Gatha.' Agatha! Is your name Agatha?" he asked the child.

"No, sir, I am Hope."

"'Gather.' Gather. That must be the word. Gather what?"

Again the invalid made a desperate attempt to speak.

"'Together.' It is 'together,'" said the little girl.

The sick man's eyes brightened, but still wore the eager, anxious look that had come into them when he first saw the children.

"What can he mean by that?" asked a bystander.

"Father, dear, do you mean for us to keep together?" asked the child.

How the sick man's eyes shone in answer!

"Then listen, father. Here, Ned! Here, Martin!" She took their hands and drew them close to her, where he could see them. "Listen, father. We promise, Ned and Martin and I, that until we are men and woman grown, we will never be parted. We promise faithfully. You tell him so, Ned; and you, Martin."

His body condemned to a living death, with the

imperishable soul still chained within, how eloquent the eyes of the father became, as he heard this promise! Then the little maid forgot her womanly dignity, forgot that strange men were by, remembered only that she was about to part with the dear father, who had been father and mother, too, since the sweet young mother closed her eyes on this world, and that this was a parting harder than that beside the coffin.

"Good-by, good-by, father, dear. Oh, father, father, if I could only stay with you! We will do the best we can. Don't trouble about us. Precious, darling father, good-by."

CHAPTER II.

WAYS AND MEANS.

The children found themselves standing on the sidewalk, with half-blinded eyes, watching the crowds go by.

All their faculties seemed dulled by the great sorrow that had come upon them. Where to go or what to do next, they did not know. They had no relatives to whom they could appeal in their need, no one closely bound by the ties of blood or of friendship, to whom it would be right and natural to apply for counsel. Their lives had been singularly bound up in each other, father and children relying upon each other for help, companionship, and advice.

They were moving down the street, and were insensibly retracing their steps to the school from which they had lately come, graduated so harshly from happy boyhood and girlhood into the great world's cares and sorrows. Soon they had reached the schoolhouse, and stood, hesitating, outside the door in the high board fence that surrounded it.

"What is the use?" said Ned. "We are through with all this. We have got to study up ways and means of living."

"Let's talk with Mr. Roberts about it," suggested Martin.

Hope had not once spoken since she left her father. She had been crying a little, silently, wiping her eyes by stealth, that the boys might not see. She followed them meekly now, as they entered the yard, which was prettily laid out, with neat walks and rows of blossoming shrubs, and a large planked playground just visible in the rear.

The schoolhouse was a tall, three-story building, plain to the very eaves. It somehow bore the look of a great factory, and I am inclined to think that the likeness extended further, for there is a great deal of machine work in our public-school system at the West, as elsewhere, and the young minds which are run through this intellectual mill are apt to come out like pieces of modern furniture: nicely seasoned, neatly joined and finished, and well up to the pattern, but lacking the individual stamp the old-fashioned cabinet-makers and school-teachers used to give.

The building had a cheery, sunshiny look. Some of the windows were open, and through them came the buzz of youthful voices, the light patter of feet, the tinkle of low-voiced bells. From one room arose a merry chorus, a little out of time and very much out of tune.

"They're going to dismiss," said Martin, and the children hastened up the walk, stepping softly, so as not to attract attention. By the time a brisk drum-beat sounded the signal for the different classes to fall into line, they had gained the Principal's private office, and, closing the door, sat down to await his coming.

Mr. Roberts gave a start as he saw the children, for he had expected to find the room vacant, as he had left it. He was a nervous man, as one may well be whose occupation is a constant draught upon all the nervous forces.

"You were called away from school this morning. Nothing wrong, I hope?"

Martin fumbled awkwardly with the fastenings of his satchel. Ned stood by the master's desk, fingering a glass paper-weight which he had often seen there, and which at another time he would never have presumed to touch. Now he lifted it as recklessly as if it had been a marble, and, holding it between his eye and the light, carelessly squinted through it.

It was an uncouth action, but it expressed, more forcibly than a more dramatic gesture, the boy's inner disturbance and indifference to trivial things.

"Why, Ned, what is the matter?" urged the master, noting how the boy's face was working. "No accident has happened to any of your family, I hope."

"There was no family but our father," said the lad in a choked voice. "Now he is"—

"Dead?" said the master, in a shocked voice.

"Worse. Paralyzed. The doctor says he will never get over it. They've taken him to the hospital—to stay."

"Why, boys, this is bad," said Mr. Roberts. "What are you going to do?"

It was noticeable that he did not include the little girl, who was standing at the window, looking down upon her young playmates as they ran blithely through the yard, on their way home to luncheon. Nobody knew it then, but Hope was at that moment saying good-by to her childhood.

"That's just the trouble," explained Ned, gathering strength as he spoke. "It has come upon us so suddenly. We don't know what to do. And we had n't any one else to talk with."

"I suppose you have small means"—

"Almost nothing," said Ned decisively, while a sudden recollection smote him: the life insurance policy, which his father had pinched himself to keep up, and which he had once confided to the boy's care, assuring him that it would provide amply for them all in case of his death. Was *he* thinking of it now, the lonely, helpless sufferer, wishing, perhaps, that it had been death that had stricken him down? He tried to put the thought from his mind.

"I suppose there are some things we could realize a little on," he said gravely; "but nothing that could begin to support us or to start us out in anyway. We shall have to go to work, Martin and I."

Mr. Roberts's face brightened.

"That's the kind of spirit that always succeeds," he said heartily. "I think we can manage it.

Probably we can hunt up places where you can go to school and work your board out of school hours."

"But we don't want to be separated. We promised father we would n't," objected Ned.

"Ah, yes, I see. But we must contrive a way for you to keep up your studies. It would be such a pity to stop now," said the teacher, gnawing his moustache and wrinkling his forehead, in a way that showed very plainly he did not at all see the way out of the young people's dilemma.

"Mr. Roberts," said Hope, coming away from the window and standing before the principal with her small hands clasped before her and her shy eyes upraised to his, "my father used to say that the most valuable part of education was what one got outside of school. Suppose we never went to school any more, but read and studied at home, and learned what we could from those about us. Or suppose that in a few years we could earn enough to take the boys through school. Would they be hurt by waiting, Mr. Roberts?"

If an oracle had found voice and spoken, the schoolmaster could not have been more surprised. Hitherto he had been thinking entirely of the boys, fine, promising fellows as he had always regarded them, and secretly regretting this check to their careers. He had even thought, with pity for them, that this young sister would be a heavy burden. She had never been counted among his brightest pupils. If he could have seen Hope bending at night over the family mending, while the boys were deep in their studies, he might have understood why she always seemed a little dull and slow at her books. But he had taken her at his own estimate, and lo! here she had risen up before him, like a fearless little woman, and was challenging his views, attempting to reverse his judgment.

"What do you suggest?" he asked calmly, a quizzical smile playing upon his face.

"I was thinking," said the girl, flushing at his tone, "that we might do better somewhere in the country. It would cost less to live in some small town than here in the city. Perhaps we might rent a place with a little ground that we could plant. We might keep chickens. And we could work for other people. Of course we couldn't earn the same as grown men and women, but then we would not need so much to eat."

Mr. Roberts listened gravely as she unfolded her plan. Then he stole a keen glance at the boys.

"And what do you say?"

He looked at Ned as he spoke. Martin was glad it was not he who had to answer, for he had a sneaking fondness for school and the playground, and the noise and whirl of the city. But Ned answered in the most resolute way, —

"I am ready for anything that will help us to keep together and to get on in the world, sir. Father always said that little Hope had more sense than both of us boys put together."

He passed his arm protectingly about his sister

for an instant. Mr. Roberts rose and took two or three turns around the room in silence. The children thought nothing strange of this proceeding, for they knew it was the master's way. When he stopped before them again, his face was animated by a new idea.

"Why don't you take up some land?" he asked.

"Take up land!" exclaimed the three in a breath.

"Yes, enter a quarter section of government land, under the homestead act."

"Why, we're not old enough," cried Ned.

"And we'd have to go away off from everywhere!" objected Martin.

"You know, Mr. Roberts, father has to stay in the hospital, under the doctor's care. It would n't be right to take him away," said Hope gently.

"If I'm not mistaken, Ned, in view of your father's hopeless incapacity, you can declare yourself the head of the family, and file upon any hundred and sixty acres of land that is open to entry," said the master. "What is more, I am very sure that across the bay and along the fruit belt of the foothills, there is some excellent land still open to settlement. How would you like to try it?"

Small need of answer. The children's faces were radiant. To be raised in a moment from the depths of poverty to the prospective ownership of a hundred and sixty acres of land — California land, with all its splendid possibilities and latent wealth — was something so magnificent that they could scarcely believe in its reality. The schoolmaster saw their exultation and tried to check it.

"It means hard work, plain living, and self-denial — years of it," he said.

"What do we care?" exclaimed Ned with enthusiasm. "It's worth it. I'd work my fingers to the bone for it."

"Only think: a home of our own!" said Hope softly.

"But where are we to get the ploughs and shovels and farming things we shall need?" asked Martin.

"Don't borrow trouble, my boy," said the master pleasantly. "Once make up your mind to accomplish any wise and worthy enterprise, and you will generally succeed. Now go home, take account of all your resources, and report to me next Saturday morning. Meanwhile, I will make some inquiries, and see if I cannot give you some practical intelligence. Hold yourselves ready for action."

CHAPTER III.

THE ABANDONED CLAIM.

It was well for the children that they had something to divide their thoughts when they entered their desolate home. The house was a neat cottage, of the type commonly occupied by San Francisco mechanics. There was a pretty little garden in front, where roses and fuchsias and flowering geraniums grew in great profusion. A narrow plank walk ran around to the side of the house, where there was a small porch, draped with honeysuckle and fragrant with its blossoms. They climbed the steps leading to this porch, and took the door key from beneath the mat, where they were in the habit of secreting it. As they did so, they noticed a basket containing meat and vegetables, their father's provision for the evening meal, and this simple testimony of his thoughtful care brought fresh pain to their hearts.

It surprised them a little to find everything within unchanged. There were his slippers, just as he had drawn them off that morning, and his morning paper, neatly folded, lay on a stand at one side of the room. Everything was in perfect order, left so by the deft hands of Biddy McGinnis, who came every forenoon to wash the dishes that had accumulated since the previous morning, and to tidy up the house. They could not afford to keep a regular servant, and this had been their father's way of lightening their home cares since their mother's death.

They came out of the house, and sitting down on the steps of the little porch, took out the luncheons they had carried in their satchels, and tried to eat; but after a weak pretense they gave up the effort, and the two younger welcomed Ned's proposal that they should follow Mr. Roberts's advice and count up their resources.

The next morning Ned stepped around to Mr. Abraham's store, and showed him the list of things that they had decided they could spare, and asked him to come over and look at them.

Mr. Abraham was the Israelite who kept the second-hand store around the corner, on Mission Street. He was a small man, with bright black eyes and shoulders that drooped forward. Mrs. Abraham was very large and stout, and stooped the other way. They had known the children ever since they came into the neighborhood, and always had a kind word for them as they passed by.

This worthy pair listened with genuine sympathy to the story Ned told. They had children of their own, and knew how to feel for other people's children.

"Mein Gott, dat iss pad!" said Mr. Abraham soberly.

"An' vwhat vill you pe doing, mein poor poys?" asked Mrs. Abraham, with unctuous kindness, while tears of honest sympathy ran down her cheeks. "Iff you likes to ko into de secont-hant pizness, now, mein huspant he peen talking of hiring a poy; he coot not gif mooch moneys, pecause de times dey iss so hart, but"—

"Vilhelmine! Vilhelmine!" interrupted her little husband in a severe voice. "Mens moost attent to deir own pizness. It iss not proper mit voomans to mettle. You go ant get some dose gookies vat you peen pakin' dis mornin', ant sent ofer to de leetle girl. Now, mein poy," turning again to Ned, "vat iss it you peen sayin', eh? You got some vernicher to sell?"

"Here is a list of the things," said Ned. "Or perhaps you would rather come over to the house, and look at the things yourself?"

"Dat is mooch petter," agreed Mr. Abraham.

Wilhelmine came in at that moment with the cookies, which Ned accepted with reluctance. Leaving the good woman to mind the store in his absence, her better if not greater half seized his hat and walked off with alacrity.

Mr. Abraham had a tender heart, but business was business, and with a large family of children of his own, their interests must be attended to first. Ned had securely reckoned upon receiving at least three fourths of the original cost of the goods he offered for sale, for the most of them were new, and all of them were well kept; but his heart sank as Mr. Abraham found moth holes in the parlor furniture, and pointed out a faded place in the carpet, and discovered scratches on the rest of the furniture, and turned the chairs upside down and the wardrobe inside out, and pronounced everything old-fashioned that was n't worn out, and everything worn-out that was n't old-fashioned.

Mr. Abraham made a list of his own, as the children pointed out the things to him. When he had finished, his list, with the prices he was willing to give, ran as follows: —

Parlor furniture	$16.00
Marble-topped table	3.50
Tapestry carpeting	7.00
Bedroom carpeting	4.00
Hatstand	6.50
Little table	1.00
Wardrobe	4.00
Parlor curtains	2.00
Dining table	5.00
Six cane-seat chairs	3.00
Garden hose	1.00
Lounge	5.00
Odds and ends	5.00
Total	$63.00

"Dat iss mooch more as de tings is vort," he said. "I haf hart vork to get mein moneys pack."

"But the things cost over two hundred dollars. Most of them are as good as new, Mr. Abraham," protested Ned.

"All right. You goes to some odder secont-hant man; den you vill see how mooch he gifs. I tell you I gifs mooch more dan anypotty else," and Mr. Abraham made a gesture as if he designed washing his hands of the whole transaction.

So the children walked back and forth through the house again, Mr. Abraham with them, singling out now this article, now that, to add to the list, and when they had finished and counted out all that they could possibly spare, the second-hand man's estimate ran up to eighty-nine dollars and some odd cents, and he only awaited their orders to come and take the goods and pay the money for them.

When they arrived at the schoolmaster's house on Saturday, they found him seated at the desk in his study, with an open letter before him.

"Well?" he said, as the boys took seats beside him.

"We acted on your advice, Mr. Roberts," replied Ned. "We made a list of all the things we had that would be useful on a ranch, and another list of all that we could spare. By selling these we can raise a little over eighty-nine dollars, less what it costs us to live while we stay here."

The schoolmaster knit his brows.

"That is very little," he said. "What have you to begin on, besides that?"

Ned pulled a memorandum from his pocket. It was very clear and concise. Mr. Roberts read:—

Working clothing enough for one year.
Cook stove.
Kitchen table.
Three chairs.
One rocker.
Two beds and bedding.
Plenty of dishes and table linen.
One small carpet.
One screen safe for food.
One meal chest, nearly full of white flour, oatmeal and corn meal, and graham flour.
Kitchen utensils.
One bureau.
One sewing machine.
One lounge.
Garden tools: rake, hoe, and spade.

"You seem to have made a very wise selection, boys," said Mr. Roberts. "But speaking of garden tools reminds me of something else. Your father was a cabinet-maker. Didn't he have a set of tools?"

"Of course he did," replied Martin quickly. "And the nicest ones you ever saw — a whole kit — everything from a brad-awl to a spirit-level!"

"Yes, he had," averred Ned. "And they hadn't been used long. It can't be more than a year since he sold his old tools and bought new ones."

"The tools would come handy for you, no doubt," said Mr. Roberts, "but it would be several years before you could handle them to advantage. A good set of tools ought to be worth somewhere from fifty to a hundred dollars," he added thoughtfully. "Have you seen anybody from the factory since?"

"No, sir," replied Ned. "We could n't expect it. The men work early and late. They never have any time to spare until Saturday night."

"I think I'll take time by the forelock and go there to-day," observed the master. "Now, boys, I have a letter here that came last night. It is from Dr. John, the friend I spoke of, who lives in the interior of Alameda County. You shall have it, word for word, as he wrote it. It is dated at his little country place."

September 5, 188–.

FRIEND ROBERTS, — Your letter of inquiry regarding government land open to settlement in this vicinity reached me to-night, and I hasten to reply.

Within a radius of ten miles of this place, a dozen or more "locations" could probably be made. These tracts are generally at a considerable elevation along the Coast Range, and are alike in character. The ground is rocky and hilly, affording fair pasturage during the winter months, but offering almost insuperable obstacles to cultivation. Here and there a fertile spot may be found, consisting of a sheltered saddle or bench, a few acres in extent; but all are open to the same drawbacks: inaccessibility and distance from any good wagon road, and therefore from market.

There is, however, one quarter section lying close to me, upon which nobody places any value, but which I should seriously consider if I were about to enter land. To explain its situation clearly, I must first make you acquainted with The Brook. Why "The Brook," I do not precisely know, but I believe there was once a dispute over its christening, and as the people could not agree on any other name, they compromised on this simple title. . . . This mountain stream rises at the summit of the Coast Range, and crosses the mountains through a picturesque cañon, coursing through our little village on its way to the Bay. Ordinarily it is a demure and well-behaved traveler, although abounding in deep pools and dangerous quicksands. In the winter time it wears a different aspect. You must know that it has for its watershed a vast area of mountain country, many hundreds of miles in extent. . . . When the winter's rains come down bravely, and clouds hover for days along the summit of the Range, The Brook is swelled by hundreds and thousands of tiny rivulets. Little by little it gathers force and volume, until it swells into a thing of terror, which sweeps down the valley with a deafening roar. When in this mood, nothing can stay it. It seizes upon giant trees, uprooting them like grasses and tossing them like babes on its bosom. It makes sallies to right and to left, snatching at fences and outbuildings that unwary farmers place too near its course, channeling inscriptions in the solid rock. Long ago people learned to give it a wide berth. Nobody would dare to build up the cañon, if, indeed, they could conveniently get there. At certain points further down the valley, the people found they had the advantage of the stream and determined to keep it, and so constructed costly iron bridges, which serve to connect sections of the valley in winter time, but which there is no traffic or population to justify up our way. Now to describe the land of which I speak: My own place borders upon The Brook at a point where the bed is full of quicksands. Just opposite lies this quarter section, a very pretty stretch of land, comprising a small crescent of level and gently sloping ground, bounded by the stream in front and the mountains on either hand, while the remainder extends up the steep hillside and embraces a thickly wooded gorge. Near as the place seems, it can only be reached by a steep trail leading back over the mountains, and connecting with a rough country road at a point some fifteen miles distant from the nearest railroad station. . . . The land was entered, some ten years ago, by a thriftless sort of fellow, who put up some rough buildings, and then gave up in disgust and abandoned the claim. His failure discouraged any one else from trying it. . . . In my judgment, the lower level is of rich alluvial soil, and could be made very productive with careful cultivation. . . . I don't know what buildings there are over there; probably there is something that could be made habitable in this accommodating climate. The little gorge ought to afford plenty of firewood. Taking it all in all, the place might be made fairly profitable, and the situation is beautiful to anybody capable of appreciating such things.

The drawbacks are most definite and uncompromising. The place is extremely difficult to reach, and once there, there would be little opportunity to get out. If your young people should go there, they must count upon leading a lonely and secluded life. They will be in a state of siege for months every winter, when the trail will be impassable.

Don't ask me whether I advise it. Everything depends on what kind of stuff they are made of. You say there is a girl; so much the worse for her and the better for them.

Yours truly,   Dr. John.

I inclose memoranda of the location, in case you should like to use it. If the children decide to come, consign them to me, and I will find some way of getting them and their belongings there.

"'Dr. John!' What a singular letter and what an odd name," remarked Martin.

"Yes," said the schoolmaster absently. "I have always fancied that he was a man with a history."

Martin looked curious, and would have followed his remarks with a question, but Ned, who had been lost in deep thought, forestalled him: —

"I will take the land," he said.

The schoolmaster looked both surprised and pleased at this decisive speech. Martin was disposed to feel somewhat aggrieved. He had expected to be consulted and to have a voice in the matter; but he hastened to sustain his dignity by giving his own vote.

"All right, Ned. I'm with you."

"I like that," said Mr. Roberts cordially, addressing Ned. "And now I am going to make another suggestion. As a rule, you know my maxim is to 'Make haste slowly;' but in this case every minute you wait is so much precious time lost. It is now nearly ten. What do you say to meeting me at the United States Land Office at eleven?"

"That will suit me, Mr. Roberts," replied Ned.

"Another thing," said the schoolmaster as he rose, eyeing the boys nervously. "I am going to bequeath to you a serious and important charge. I am going to give you my heifer calf."

That heifer calf! The boys forgot their dignity and burst into hearty laughter. The pretty little Jersey, the gift of a devoted pupil, had been the master's plague and Nemesis for months past. It had drawn him into more scrapes than Mary's little lamb had beguiled its mistress. It was forever escaping from his own adjoining yard into the school grounds, frightening timid children, and driving bold ones wild with delight. It had lunched one day on the experimental garden planted by the botany class. It had browsed on school satchels and hats and coats in the entry. It had once been imprisoned in the principal's room by some mischievous urchins, and, escaping, wandered into a class-room and greeted some visiting directors with a loud "Baa-aa-aa!" and then had shamelessly proclaimed its ownership by sticking its nose into its master's pocket to find some hidden sweets. It had brought him into disgrace with the Board, and narrowly escaped becoming the subject of litigation in the courts. It had even now helped him into one more scrape, for there in the open doorway stood the donor of the calf, a handsome, curly-headed boy, his face red with vexation.

"If you don't want Beauty, Mr. Roberts, I'll find somebody who does. I think you might have had the politeness to tell me so, instead of joking about it with the other boys. As for you, Ned, and you, Martin, you dare to lay one finger to that calf, and I'll"—

"Thomas Bateman, be silent. Go and sit in that chair. I will talk with you later," commanded Mr. Roberts, in the tone of authority that no one ever dared disobey. "Now, boys, you may go; but don't fail to meet me at the Land Office at eleven, sharp."

CHAPTER IV.

THE HEAD OF A FAMILY.

AFTER a short talk with his refractory visitor, Mr. Roberts betook himself to the large furniture factory in the lower portion of the city. He was referred to the tall foreman, who proved to be a working partner of the firm.

"Oh, yes, those poor little shavers of Austin's!" he said, folding his arms and looking troubled. "It's a hard case. The men are going to do something for them to-night. Saturday's pay-day, you know."

"You can't reach them in that way," said the schoolmaster with decision.

"Eh?" said the foreman, looking puzzled.

"The boys are young, but they have character," insisted Mr. Roberts. "They don't want charity. They mean to take care of themselves."

"But we can't see a man drop right down among us, and not raise a finger to help his family, — and a pack of poor little youngsters at that."

"Then help them in a different way. Mr. Austin has a chest of tools here, has he not?"

"Yes, sir, and in the best of order. A good workman always takes good care of his tools."

"Can't you sell them at a good price? The boys need money. You could help them in that way, without hurting their self-respect."

The foreman excused himself for a moment, and consulted with others of the firm. When he came back he brought a check for a hundred dollars.

"Shall we make this payable to you, Mr. Roberts?"

"Make it payable to Ned — Edward Austin. He is the head of the family now, and we must look upon him as a man henceforth."

Ned did not look at all like a man or the head of a family, but like a very slight, careworn boy, when the young people joined their friend, on the steps of the Treasury Building.

In the Land Office, at the counter where entries were made, the clerk was busily talking with a lady, and excused himself to Mr. Roberts with an apologetic word. Martin possessed himself of a pamphlet lying on the counter, while Ned got his data ready, and anxiously awaited his turn.

The lady who was talking with the clerk appeared to be an old acquaintance. She was a pretty woman, and stylishly dressed.

"Now do advise me!" she exclaimed in a coaxing tone. "Would you preëmpt it or homestead it? Which is the least trouble?"

"If you preëmpt it, it will cost you a dollar and a quarter an acre, and you'll have to live on it for six months. If you homestead it, the fees and commissions only amount to twenty-two dollars:

sixteen when you enter it, and six more on final proof. But you'll have to live on it for five years."

"Five years? You don't mean it!" cried the lady, with a little scream of horror. "Wouldn't once a week or twice a month do?"

"You might make it 'do,'" said the clerk, with a meaning smile. "But you'd have to run risks. Somebody might be watching."

"Five years! Oh, that would never do," said the lady impatiently. "What does government suppose I want to take up its old land for? I want the money for it."

"So do most people," said the clerk, with another expressive smile.

"Now preëmpting sounds more sensible," continued the lady; "though how in the world I'm going to bury myself there for six months I don't see. Say, don't you suppose if I dress up a dummy and set it at the window, I can come down to the city in disguise every week or so, to go to the theatre and do a little shopping?"

"Woman's wit will probably circumvent all obstacles," replied the clerk.

"And then, at the end of six months, I'd have to pay — let me see: a hundred and sixty times one dollar and twenty-five cents. Oh, dear, I've such a poor head for figures. How much would that be?"

"Two hundred dollars."

"I'd have to pay two hundred dollars. And I

can get thirty dollars an acre for the land as soon as I get the title. And thirty times one hundred and sixty — why, it's forty-eight hundred. And take away the two hundred dollars, leaves forty-six hundred dollars. That's not a bad speculation after all!" And she laughed triumphantly.

".Let me see your forms, or whatever you call them. Oh, if you please!" extending her hand for Martin's open book, on whose page she caught sight of the clause she wished to see.

"But see what it says here," cried Martin, pointing to the affidavit. "'*I do solemnly swear . . . nor have I settled upon and improved said land to sell the same on speculation, but in good faith;'*" —

"Oh, nonsense!" exclaimed the lady hastily.

"But don't you have to take your solemn oath you haven't?" questioned the boy.

"What a little goose!" laughed the lady, recovering herself. "Why, everybody does so. People are doing it every day. Thousands and thousands of acres are entered that way every year, and every one knows it."

"And isn't swearing to something that isn't true, perjury?" insisted Martin stoutly.

"That's enough, young man," hastily interposed the clerk. "It's all a matter of form. Everybody understands it."

Meanwhile, somebody had been looking up the boys' claim, and found it open to entry.

"Of course your residence is already on the land?

You know that is necessary in entering a homestead claim?" said the man, addressing Mr. Roberts.

"No, sir, I was not aware of that. This is a new complication, Ned. You'll have to move up there first, and then come down to the city and make the entry. This is the young man who expects to enter the land," explained Mr. Roberts.

The entry clerk caught the words, and looked at the boys with surprise tinctured with disfavor, for Martin's blunt speeches had not aroused the good will of the office.

"You don't mean to say that you are twenty-one years old, young man?" he demanded, eying Ned with suspicion.

"No, sir; but I am the head of the family."

"Father and mother both dead, eh?"

"The mother is dead," interposed Mr. Roberts in a low voice.

"And the father?"

"Here is the physician's certificate, showing that he is hopelessly incapacitated."

"I can't think of permitting such a thing," said the clerk harshly. "Never had such a case before to my knowledge. The Department would never allow it."

"Well, boys, we shall have to give it up," said the schoolmaster sadly.

Ned came forward, his face pale, but his eyes resolute, making one last, brave stand.

"I want to see the Land Registrar himself," he demanded.

The clerk held a hurried consultation with his superior. The latter finally came forward, his fine face lighted with interest.

"You want to take up land, eh? Turn rancher? What for?"

"To make a home and earn a living for my brother and sister and myself," replied Ned promptly.

"Not afraid of hard work? Don't mind leaving the city?"

"No, sir."

"Well, I have two boys at home, and I wish they had half your pluck," said the gentleman. "Now as to this application of yours. It's irregular, I must own. But I can't see why it shouldn't hold. If a man runs away and deserts his family, his widow, and presumably his minor child, in the case of her death, may declare themselves heads of the family, and enter land accordingly. When an honest man is stricken down by disease, I can't see why members of his family shouldn't be entitled to the same privilege. It may arouse some discussion in Washington, but if you can afford to take the risk, I think we can and will. You go up and settle on the land, and then enter it in the office of the county clerk of Alameda County. If he makes any objection, refer him to me."

CHAPTER V.

TOM'S APOLOGY.

THERE was nothing left for the children to do but to prepare their simple possessions for shipment. Nearly all of their little circle of friends testified their sympathy and good will in some practical manner. Biddy McGinnis brought a coop containing a hen and a brood of chickens. The grocery man at the corner pressed upon them some packages of garden seeds. Even Mr. Abraham, impelled in part, no doubt, by his wife, brought to each of the boys a stout suit of overalls and jumper for farm work, when he came to take away the furniture they had sold him. Their landlord returned to them half of the month's rent, which had been paid in advance. A thriftless mechanic, one of their father's fellow-workmen, came up one day, leading a half-starved, broken-down old horse, and explained that he wanted them to accept the animal in settlement of a debt of twenty dollars that he owed their father.

"If you can make any use of this old mare," he said, "you're welcome to her. She's old and banged up, and she looks bad because she's been straw-fed; but she's sound, and gentle as a kitten."

The boys accepted the bony old mare, although they were almost ashamed to drive her down to the ferry; but they reasoned that after all she was a horse, capable of work, and they secretly hoped good pasturage might improve her.

A few evenings before they left, they had a surprise. They were startled by the sound of a noisy altercation at the gate, then a stampede up the walk.

Two voices, a boy's and a man's, were heard outside; then there was a clatter as if a squad of infantry had raced upon the little porch. There were gruff murmurs and smothered laughter.

The boys, thoroughly alarmed, sprang to the door and flung it open.

On the porch a man and a boy were wrestling with something very strong and very active, and very wild and unmanageable; something that was spotted, dun-color and white, and had eyes like a fawn, and long silken ears that pricked up as the door opened, in a very knowing fashion.

"That'll do, Jim," said the boy, in the tone of one accustomed to giving orders. "I've got her now. You can go."

The man lifted his hat to the children, and disappeared into the darkness.

"Baa-aa-aa!"

Surely they knew the familiar call.

"Beauty?" said Ned, amazed.

"That's what's the matter," replied Tom Bateman, for it was he, avoiding Ned's eye as he secured the rope to one of the posts. "Afraid you might forget her — knew you were awful busy. Thought I'd bring her along myself."

But Ned was a boy, too, and he still smarted under a sense of indignity at the savage threats young Bateman had made at the schoolmaster's house the previous week. Such an offense was not to be condoned in a moment.

"I don't want your calf," he said bluntly. "Keep her yourself."

Just then Hope appeared at the door, drawing back shyly as she recognized the visitor.

"Good-evening, Hope," said Tom, smiling.

Hope accepted this greeting with a little nod, and stepped out to caress Beauty, who gave a friendly bleat at sight of her.

Something had happened the Saturday before; something that Hope had not told the boys.

After they had left the house, she had gone out on the back steps to have the "good cry" that she had been promising herself, the only relief that her overcharged heart could find. She had been holding back all the week, and the tears rained down thick and fast, while her slight form shook with the sobs she could no longer control. Sitting, or rather lying there, with her head pillowed on her arms, she was unconscious of everything about her.

A moment later Tom Bateman came along the walk at the side of the house, and opened the gate in the tall lattice-work that separated the front yard from the back. He thrust his head through the opening, and called out, in a cautious voice, as if not sure what sort of reception he might meet:

"Boys!"

Hope raised her head and recognized him, and tried to recover her self-command, but could not. Dropping her face again upon her arms, she sobbed as if her heart would break.

"Why, Hope!" said Tom.

He was a big boy, in class A, of the first Grammar grade, and she was a little girl, grades and grades below him; but from the time he had first seen her she had reminded him of a little sister he had lost, and whom, for love's sake and the pain the memory cost him, he had tried hard to forget.

But now he sat down on the step beside her, and drew the little girl into his arms, and made a clumsy effort to quiet and console her.

"Don't cry," he said. "It's a terrible thing, I know. Mr. Roberts has been telling me about it. But you can't help matters by crying. You'll just take away the boys' pluck."

"But — the boys — are n't — here!" sobbed the child.

"But I am, and I can't stand it. Do stop, Hope! You'll kill yourself, crying so. Would that make it easier for them or your father?"

He had succeeded in quieting her at last, and he dried her eyes with a handkerchief not very immaculate, and before he left wrung from her a reluctant promise that she would not cry any more.

"When you feel like it, just tear round the house and bang things about, and make other people feel bad. That's the way I do."

Hope laughed.

" But don't tell the boys," she implored him.

The consciousness of this innocent secret embarrassed them both at this next meeting; but it made Tom all the more determined to establish pleasant relations with the brothers of the little girl who had sobbed out her sorrows in his arms.

"Don't be spunky, Ned," urged Tom in a low voice. "I did n't know — I had n't heard anything about — why you left school, you know. Besides, Beauty really is a terrible nuisance. She's getting dangerous. Her horns are growing. You don't want her to go to the slaughter house. The 'governor' declares he'll send her there if he finds her round another day."

Ned could but own that he would not like to have the pretty creature meet such a tragical fate.

There was a tone of filial indifference in Tom's reference to his father that neither of the other children could understand, having been reared under widely different conditions. Tom Bateman was the type of many a San Francisco boy, whose father was given over to business speculations and his mother to society. It sometimes occurred to Tom that he was not very well acquainted with his parents. It is needless to say that no thought of this came to either of the boys as they stood on the steps of the narrow portico, the one eager, apologetic, determined; the other reluctant and wavering.

"There's no question but that Beauty would ruin Mr. Roberts if he kept her three months longer. The directors have got their eye on her, and either she'll have to go, or he'll be fired. If she could only get out in the country and be put on grass or alfalfa, there'd be some reason in it. But when it comes to keeping her on schoolbooks and hats, and satchels, and choice roses, and orchids — she cleaned out all the orchids in our conservatory yesterday (you see Mr. Roberts made me take her home," he confessed, in an embarrassed aside), — "she's — she's ruination. Hold on! She's got your handkerchief now."

So she had, and was calmly chewing it, with the anticipation of a new and delicate cud by and by. The shout that went up at this discovery restored good feeling between the boys, and emboldened Tom to discharge another errand, no act of atonement in this instance, but a pure, unselfish impulse to give a lift to the boy friends whose way must henceforth be an uphill climb.

"Look here, boys," he cried, kneeling down and fitting a key to the lock of the large, solid-looking box the man had put down on the porch, "can't you make some use of these things out on your ranch?"

He threw up the lid as he spoke, disclosing what had been a well-appointed chest of boy's tools, of excellent manufacture, but in sad disorder.

"Oh, Tom! We couldn't think of such a thing. You'll want them yourself," exclaimed both boys in a breath.

"No, I don't. Haven't got the least mechanical genius in the world. Can't drive a nail without hitting my fingers. You'll find them in an awful mess, though. I broke the bull-nose plane the day I got them, trying to scrape a nail out of my boot. And last week I turned a screw on my bicycle with the chisel, and nicked a piece out of it. Now, boys, I must be going. Success to you on the ranch! Good-by, Hope. I'm coming up to see you all some day."

He was off before they could say a word of thanks.

Before they left, Ned took a very practical and sensible step. He went to a locksmith close by, a curious old man who had the reputation of being a veritable jack-at-all-trades, and served a brief apprenticeship in various simple crafts with which he foresaw that it might be valuable to be acquainted. He learned how to set a pane of glass, to sharpen tools, to file and set a saw, to hang a door, and to do innumerable other things that to procure done is the torment of the average farmer.

CHAPTER VI.

THE MAN WITH A HISTORY.

They said good-by to their little home, to their few friends, to the very streets their young feet had trod since infancy. They paid one last sorrowful visit to the hospital, and stood by their father's bedside, endeavoring to make him understand their project, turning away with full hearts as they thought they saw an expression of approval in the patient eyes. Now they were on the cable cars, gliding down Market Street to the ferry, so absorbed in their own thoughts that they did not see the tangle of vehicles that thronged the streets, all converging to a focus at the water front. And now they were on the boat, three small units in a vast, bustling, cosmopolitan crowd, each factor intent upon its own interests and purposes. And now they were on the train, speeding to a new home and a new life.

Their goods, along with Beauty and the coop of chickens, had been shipped the day before, consigned to Dr. John. It was very natural, as the train passed Oakland and Fruit Vale, and began to move through the open country, that each of the young travelers should be thinking of this same

Dr. John, each in a different manner and from a different point of view. They burst into speech almost at the same time.

"I hope we shall like him," said Ned.

"I wonder if he will like us," said Hope.

"If he'll only tell us stories of his adventures!" cried Martin.

Ned and Hope smiled at this outburst. Ever since Mr. Roberts had dropped the remark that Dr. John was a man with a history, Martin had been feeding his boyish imagination with every sort of wild conception wherein the doctor figured as the hero.

But Oakland was ten miles behind them, and they were coming to a place where a spur of the foothills descended, in gentle undulations, to the level of the valley. The hills loomed higher and approached ever nearer, until they took on the dignity of young mountains. Little farmhouses were seen along their base and halfway up their slopes, and now and then an ambitious building, with elaborate grounds, where semitropical shrubs and fruits flourished.

The train slackened speed, and came to a standstill, and the conductor shouted a name that caused the boys to grasp their valise and bundles, and Hope to hug closer the flower-pot in which she had planted slips from their small city garden.

The brothers ran lightly down the steps, Ned turning to help Hope down, while Martin looked eagerly around.

They found themselves on a broad platform surrounding a neat station house. The depot was a long red building, and at the further end was a garden, through gaps in whose high hedge glimpses could be had of rosebushes and of orange-trees laden with half-matured fruit. There were many people on the platform, and Martin scanned them critically to find among them some impressive figure, the man for whom he was looking : "the man with a history."

It was hard to decide upon him. There were porters and train hands, trundling heavy trucks and shouting hoarse orders. There were brisk-looking travelers coming and going. There was a young man taking leave of his young wife, and an old gentleman welcoming home his old wife. At one side of the platform a ranchman, wearing a gray felt hat, who had just stepped out of a light wagon, was trying to calm his horse, a noble bay with a long, arched neck and a beautiful eye, who shivered with terror at every puff of the engine, and seemed possessed with an uncontrollable desire to leap forward upon the platform and dash herself against her iron rival.

The children forgot all about the doctor, as they watched the calm, sympathetic control that the farmer exercised over the horse. Every time the animal plunged forward it found itself checked by his vice-like grasp upon the bridle. Then he would stroke it gently, and seem to reason with it, and quiet it with soothing words.

Just then the door of the refreshment room attached to the depot opened, — the boys afterwards learned that this was merely another name for the barroom, — and a tall, distinguished-looking man came out wiping his lips. He was dressed in black, and had a fierce black mustache, and carried himself with great dignity. In one hand was a gold-headed cane, in the other a small black morocco case.

Here was the model hero of romance. Martin's eyes sparkled. Ned and Hope beheld him with sinking hearts. Something in the dark, handsome face aroused in them a nameless repulsion.

The tall gentleman caught sight of the farmer struggling with the spirited horse. Several bystanders had by this time gathered around horse and master, and each offered some friendly advice. The tall stranger joined them. He also had a piece of counsel to offer : —

"What's the use of fooling with an animal in that fashion?" he demanded impatiently. "You take a stout whip and lay it over him, — raise the welts on his back, — and you won't have any more trouble with him."

"That isn't my way, doctor," said the farmer quietly.

At last the animal yielded to the firm and gentle control, and stood perfectly still, only shivering slightly as the engine, with one wild whistle and snort, thundered off down the steel track. She watched the flying train until it rounded a curve, then gave an apologetic whinny, and laid her nose on her master's shoulder, docile as a kitten.

The tall gentleman turned away with a sneering expression on his face.

"Dr. John!"

It was Martin, who gave a quick step forward and hailed him.

"Here, my boy. Where are the rest of you?"

A hearty voice, with a ring of honest welcome. Martin stopped short, and Ned and Hope looked pleasantly bewildered, for — wonder of wonders — it was the ranchman who spoke, and who now came cordially forward, relieving them of their burdens, and bidding them jump into the two-seated wagon, while he went off to see about their luggage.

Martin, smarting under the sense of his error, looked critically at Dr. John, and saw only a man of medium height and slender figure, who moved and spoke and acted precisely like other men. Under the gray felt hat appeared the face of a man of forty-odd years, very bright when he was speaking, and very sober in repose.

There was not the least suggestion of the hero about him, and Martin felt defrauded. So this wonderful Dr. John was only an everyday, ordinary man, who could be grave or gay, silent or talkative, gentle or severe, as the occasion demanded.

Ned helped his sister into the wagon, but remained standing on the platform.

It was evident that Dr. John was a general favorite, from the friendly greetings he received as he moved along the platform. Some of the loiterers, mostly villagers of respectability and farmers looking after shipments of produce, drew near and addressed friendly inquiries to the children. They seemed to be at once adopted into the little community, because they were Dr. John's charges.

"What is it, Ned?" said Dr. John, as he came up and saw the boy's waiting attitude.

This way of addressing them by their Christian names seemed to place the children on a near and friendly footing from the first.

"I must have a freight bill to pay. I would like to settle it now," Ned replied.

The children could not understand the merriment that this remark seemed to arouse among the bystanders, and which appeared to be directed at a stout, bustling man near by.

"Here's the freight agent," said the doctor genially. "Hatton, have you any bill against these young people?"

"Dr. John, this is too bad," replied the man called Hatton.

"But the waybill," insisted Ned. "They told me in the city that they always made out duplicates, and that it would be sure to reach here before the freight."

"Ned," said the doctor solemnly, "that calf of yours is a financier. She breakfasted off from her own freight bill."

"And all the others that I had in my pocket," confessed the agent.

The children could not help but laugh. It was so like Beauty.

"Young man," said a small, bright-eyed elderly gentleman in the garb of a farmer, but with the face of an old-time poet, addressing Ned, "what will you take for that calf? I can't imagine any better way of getting even with this railroad company for its extortions than to own that animal."

"I'm very sorry, sir," Ned contrived to say to the freight agent.

"Oh, never mind," said that official, glad to escape from being the butt of a practical joke, as any self-respecting man must be. "Don't give yourself any concern. I've sent down to the city for a new consignment of bills, but the sooner you get that little beast of yours out to pasture the better"—

"For the railroad company?" suggested the bright-eyed old farmer.

But the doctor had already turned away, and the fleet mare was bearing them swiftly over the smooth road and past the village, which was little more than a trading post for the surrounding country. A turn in the road brought them in sight of a noble cañon, whose mountainous gateway seemed to have been cleft asunder by some plutonic force.

Martin asked one question on the road.

"Dr. John, who was that tall, dark man who spoke to you about the horse,— the one you called 'doctor'?"

"He? Oh, he is a sort of itinerant dentist," replied Dr. John carelessly. "We don't think very highly of him about here. He gambles, and gets drunk, and beats his wife."

"Oh!" said Martin, greatly crestfallen.

All of the land they saw was under cultivation, the most of it being in orchards and vineyards. Although it was the last of September, there was still an abundance of fruit everywhere. There were trees laden with red and yellow apples; late peach-trees bent beneath their golden burdens; fig-trees sheltering great purple lobes under their abundant foliage; the russet of pears, the yellow of quinces, the dull greens and browns of almond and walnut-husks, were everywhere seen. In the vineyards stood large wagons, and stacks of boxes and groups of busy Chinamen told of the vintage at hand.

At length they turned into a place evidently much less extensive and important than its neighbors, but which somehow had a different and distinctive look: perhaps it was because of the background of hills, rising so majestically behind it; possibly it was the fringe of forest trees at one side, or the avenue of grand old sycamores leading straight from the entrance to the door. The entrance itself was something to be studied and marveled over. It was a high rustic arch, and there were rude letters above. The children spelled them out: "S-O-M-B-R-A."

"'Sombra.' What does that mean?" asked Martin.

"It is only a fancy,—the name I call my place. It is the Spanish for *shadow*, and you see I am in the shadow of the hills," answered Dr. John evasively.

The Shadow! Ned felt at once that the name had some deeper meaning.

They looked with interest on the garden through which they were passing, and which was unlike any they had ever seen before. There were none of the geometrical lines and stiff, conventional ways that possess most California gardens like a blight. This was a genuine old-fashioned garden, under a new-fashioned clime and in a new-fashioned land. Rose hedges raised a defense of thorn and flower about the stretches of green lawn. Sweet-scented white and purple violets fringed their margin. Castilian roses, tea roses, Luxembourg, Jacqueminot, Maréchal Niel, Cloth-of-gold, Gold-of-Ophir, Safrano, Bon Silene, La Marque roses, rioted everywhere and filled the air with their fragrance. There were tree-like fuchsias, and great clumps of pampas grass, and a hollow filled with wonderful varieties of flower-de-luce, of melting colors; and there was a deep pond where goldfish glanced and the pond-lily bloomed.

The house was a neat frame structure, so lost in vines that it was impossible to follow its outlines, but it had a strangely silent and deserted look.

Dr. John drew up at a side porch and went into the house, soon reappearing with a covered basket.

CHAPTER VII.

CROSSING THE RUBICON.

"Now," said the doctor gayly, "we must proceed to the claim. But how do you suppose I am going to get you across the Rubicon, and why don't you ask after your freight? How do you know that I have n't confiscated it, and may be even now leading you into some dangerous pitfall?"

He was driving down a shaded road at the rear of the house as he spoke.

"You look as if you could be trusted," said Hope quaintly.

Ned laughed boyishly at this rejoinder, but Martin saw Dr. John give a quick, strange glance at the little girl.

They soon came to the bank of a beautiful stream, with tall sycamores and bending willows gracing either margin. Beyond, on the further side, was disclosed a view that filled them with delight, for there, on a gentle slope which seemed to be hollowed out of the mountains, bounded by steep hills, and looking like a mammoth amphitheatre rent in twain, was their own dear home to be. They had a glimpse of some rough dwellings, then they heard a low, contented " Moo," and saw Beauty but a few rods below them, grazing happily away, for the first time in her life, on legitimate fodder. The children sprang out of the wagon, and the horse was tied to a tree.

"Why, Dr. John, here's something that looks like a raft," cried Ned, bending over and looking in the shadows of the willow near by.

"It is a raft," replied the doctor, "or at least it tries hard to be one. It has a good deal of business before it, and we must have confidence in it, or perhaps it will founder and go down. I think it will carry everything but your horse. He is welcome to quarters in my stable until Ned finds time to take him round by the hill trail."

As the children ran up to the pretty calf, they noticed that close to the bank of the stream, beneath a clump of alders, stood their modest packing cases.

The boys at once threw off their coats and went to work, and while Dr. John held the raft against the shore, they lifted some small articles of furniture upon it, until the doctor declared that its capacity was exhausted.

"This reminds me of some of the makeshifts in war times," observed the doctor pleasantly, as he seized a stout pole, and made ready to push off from shore.

"Were you ever a soldier?" cried Martin eagerly.

"Yes; after a fashion. Now jump aboard, Ned, and unload on the other side."

Back and forth the little craft moved, until everything inanimate was at length safely across, and there remained, besides the human passengers, one article of very animate freight, which promised some difficulty in handling.

For Beauty came aboard with a leap and a bound that almost swamped the raft, and sprang hither and thither, from one side to the other, to smell of the water, and even to refresh herself with a small draught of the crystal liquid. Once fairly launched upon her voyage, however, she behaved like an old and experienced sailor, and made the trip with great dignity, albeit she was plainly consumed with curiosity to know what it all meant.

Little Hope was the last passenger, and before he handed her on board, the doctor ran up to the wagon and lifted out the covered basket he had put in at the house. Hope was very timid, and she feared the water, but she was careful not to scream out when the raft made a sudden lunge, or to do anything that might make the doctor regard her as a drawback to the boys, as she could not help feeling Mr. Roberts had done.

"You'll come up with us, Dr. John?" asked Ned, as the doctor handed Hope ashore with grave courtesy.

"Not now, Ned. You will have to explore the place alone. I have some patients that I must be off to see. Don't attempt to do too much to-day. Your goods are perfectly safe where they are. If you cannot make yourselves comfortable for the night — Oh, well! I shall be over to see how you are doing."

Was it any wonder that the children could hardly wait to see him off, before starting out on their investigations? Hand in hand, they climbed The Brook's steep bank, leading Beauty by her rope. Then they paused, dismayed by the sight before them.

Their way was barred by a forest of tall mustard stalks, twelve to fifteen feet in height and an inch or so in diameter, dry and scorched by the long summer's heat, and crowned with dry pods that rattled when they were touched, and showered their seeds down on the parched vegetation underfoot.

With great discomfort and considerable difficulty they threaded this miniature forest, starting all sorts of wild things as they went on. Cotton-tail rabbits fled before them. Gophers stuck their heads out of the ground, and viewed them with jewel-like eyes, then noiselessly retreated to their underground preserves. Large gray ground squirrels sat up on their haunches, with bushy tails curled gracefully around them and wee forepaws dropped downward as if in mimic curtsey, but scampered off at their approach. Flocks of birds arose from their feeding grounds, and lizards rustled through the dead leaves.

When they had advanced a few rods they were surprised to find a narrow, open trail, where the ground was bare and packed hard, as if by daily tread. From its direction, this trail apparently led from the buildings to the stream. They stopped short, a little excited, and looked apprehensively at each other.

"What if some one should be living there: some hermit or crazy person," suggested Martin, who was addicted to sensational theories.

"Nonsense!" exclaimed Ned. "It is probably some wild thing, — a coon or a coyote."

When they had gone about a hundred yards they came out of the mustard field, and saw before them an old adobe cottage, so clumsily built and so badly crumbled away in places that even Ned's brave spirit sank at the thought of attempting to make it habitable.

It was a low structure, long and narrow, with the front door under the eaves, and flanked by one and two windows, on either side. Beside it was a tall Monterey cypress, and before it stood a pair of pepper trees, through whose fern-like foliage the air and sunshine played, while at either end of the rough little porch, where some careless hand had doubtless planted them years before, were pink climbing roses of luxurious growth.

The children tied the calf to the cypress, and bent their footsteps towards the house. It seemed strange to them that the front door should be ajar, but they wondered no longer when they saw that the thumb-latch was broken. What dismayed them as they climbed the rickety steps and entered the front room was the confusion of tracks that went before them, and seemed to wander aimlessly over the floor.

The room in which they found themselves was about twenty-four feet long and fourteen feet wide, with a solid floor and walls ceiled with rough boards. There was a rude fireplace at one side, but it was poorly constructed, and the space within was filled with crumbling brick.

The chimney was built out into the room, and had no pretense at a mantel; but the ledges of brick, where the fire arch narrowed into the flue, still held pieces of broken clay pipes, some rusty nails, and an old harness ring.

Behind this room was an open door leading into a little "lean-to" kitchen, which a fastidious housekeeper might have called stifling and stuffy, and many other disagreeable names; but our little housewife looked cheerfully into it, and declared that it would be nice and snug and easy to work in, when it should be cleaned out and fitted up. Ned observed that there was a stovepipe hole in the wall at one side, and drawing a rule from his pocket took its height and measurement, with an eye to business.

One more room waited to be explored. This opened off from the front room, and had a window half wreathed in by the climbing roses. As they took their way towards it, they were startled to hear a movement within, as of some heavy body dragged along the floor.

Three young hearts leaped. Three youthful

faces turned pale. Ned thought of the mysterious trail down to the Brook. Martin recalled ghost stories he had read. Hope gave a little cry of horror : —

"Oh, boys, don't go in. If — if it should be — a tramp!"

CHAPTER VIII.

DISCOVERY.

But Ned had a responsibility to sustain, as the sworn head of the family, and he pushed the half open door wide, and boldly looked in.

"I declare," he said, "if it isn't a dog!"

And so it was: a gaunt Newfoundland, who seemed in the last stages of want and despair. He was crouched on the floor, with his nose resting on his paws, and as he saw the young faces at the door he lifted his head and gave one prolonged howl. The dismal sound seemed to hold volumes of misery and pain.

"Poor fellow!" cried Ned, dropping beside him and patting his head; a caress to which the dog responded with a feeble whine, making an effort to get up, but falling back exhausted.

"He is hurt. He drags one leg after him," exclaimed Martin.

"It is an old hurt," asserted Ned, examining the maimed leg. "It has been broken or crushed, and stiffened up all out of shape. I believe the poor fellow is starving. Let us go and bring our lunch, Martin, and get some water from The Brook."

Leaving Hope with the dog, the boys hastened

back to where they had left the valise, and getting a tin pail from one of the boxes filled it with water. As they observed the doctor's basket, they remembered his parting injunction, and, opening it, found it contained a large bowl of delicious strawberries, a paper bag filled with sugar, a lot of fresh rolls, some cold meat, and a large loaf of cake, — provisions enough for a day or more.

The little girl was still sitting by the dog when they returned. He had stretched himself out upon one side, and laid one great paw on her dress. He looked up beseechingly as the boys came into the room, and they hastened to answer his dumb prayer with a dish of water, which he lapped up eagerly. Then they fed him small pieces of bread, which he caught at greedily and swallowed at a gulp, begging for more and more, until he finally sat up and tried to wag his bushy tail, in humble acknowledgment of their kindness. It sweetened their own meal to feel that they had brought relief to this unfortunate animal, and this little deed of mercy seemed to bless their first entrance into their new home.

"Now, Martin, suppose we go down and begin carrying up the things. If we work alive, I'll warrant we'll get up everything we need before night. Hope, you can stay up here or go down with us, just as you like."

"Oh, I'll stay here and tidy up a little," declared the young sister brightly. "I'll sweep down a few of these cobwebs and brush off the floors, and it will do nicely for to-night."

But Hope turned pale, even as she spoke.

"Oh, Ned. What shall I do?"

"What is it, little sister?" cried Ned with real concern.

"It is terrible. I don't know what we can do. I left the broom hanging on its nail in the city."

This oversight did not seem half as tragical to the boys as it did to the small housewife.

"Well, that's good!" "What a situation!" "Worse than 'Twelve miles from a lemon,'" were their merry comments.

"Don't you worry, little woman," said Ned. "I've read of the birch brooms our Puritan grandmothers used. There's that Monterey cypress. It needs trimming badly. Mart, you hunt up a good stick for a handle, and I'll get the rest ready."

Bough after bough fell before the sharp-bladed jackknife, and by the time Martin reappeared with an old hoe handle, Ned had fished a ball of string from his pocket and commenced to bind the green boughs, layer after layer, in true scientific fashion, about the end. In little more time than it takes to tell it, Hope was in possession of a genuine broom, very primitive in shape and not quite as efficient as one of the modern kind, but which was still invaluable at that moment.

The boys worked like Trojans, and while the sun was still high had succeeded in transporting all of the smaller articles to the house, but when it came to the stove, they were for a moment disheartened.

"We can never carry it that distance, and over the rough ground," said Ned decidedly. "We shall have to contrive a way."

Sending Martin to help Hope to place the furniture in the house, Ned set to work with hatchet and tools, and cutting down a young sapling that stood by the bank of the stream, and knocking up some of the heavier cases in which their goods had been packed, he constructed a stout little sled. Martin was called back; together the boys succeeded in placing the stove upon it, and harnessing himself to the rope he had tied to the bar across the front, with Martin pushing behind, Ned started for the house. In a short time they had the stove in place, a bright fire burning, and their evening meal before them.

When this was eaten, they hastened to make up beds and to prepare for the night's rest. Before retiring, they all stepped out of doors to take a last look at the mountains, even more beautiful by moonlight, which seemed to wrap them in a solemn silence broken only by the music of The Brook below.

They went to bed that night weary of body, but light of heart. Six willing hands, three brave hearts, an old horse, a little heifer calf, a few of the homeliest articles of household furniture, and the prospective ownership of a hundred and sixty acres of government land, was the sum of their possessions. It was not much. To some it may seem a hazy capital to start upon ; but is there another country on the face of the globe where such possibilities are open to the children of a poor mechanic ?

CHAPTER IX.

A TOUR OF EXPLORATION.

THEY awoke in the morning to the sound of a loud halloo, which seemed to come from the direction of The Brook. How many times it had already been repeated they could not guess.

Sending up an answering shout, the boys hurried on their clothes, and were soon on their way to the stream.

Dr. John had been unable to fulfill his half-made promise to return and give them his assistance the afternoon before, for he had been called off a long distance into the country, and had not returned until late in the evening. The thought of the children, in that isolated place, thrown entirely on their own resources, had worried him not a little. With the earliest light of dawn he had arisen, and, not waiting for his breakfast, hastened to The Brook and taken passage for the other side. They found him standing on the bank and looking about him in bewilderment.

"Where are your goods, and where did you sleep last night?" he demanded of the boys, as soon as they came in sight. He had quite expected to find the young people camping out beside the stream and cooking over an open campfire.

"Oh, Ned and I got everything up to the house yesterday," replied Martin indifferently.

"Well done, boys," said the doctor aloud. His inward comment was still more cordial. "Three hundred yards at least, uphill, through a thicket of weeds and brush. Plucky fellows. They'll do!" was what he said to himself.

"Well, how do things look? I suppose you've been all over the place."

"Why, no, sir," said Ned. "There was too much to do yesterday. We saved that for to-day."

Another unspoken compliment, not less cordial than the first, passed through the doctor's mind.

"Hope is up, and has a fire. She's got ahead of us this morning, Martin," exclaimed Ned, pointing to a breath of blue smoke curling up from the low cottage as they approached it.

Sure enough, as they neared the house, the little girl, her face shining, and with a neat gingham apron drawn over her woolen dress, came out to meet them and to extend a smiling welcome to the doctor.

"Hope," said Dr. John, "can't you give me a cup of coffee and a mouthful of bread? I'm hungry."

"Certainly, Dr. John. I shall be glad to," said Hope, trying hard to disguise the shyness she felt at exposing their simple ways of life to a stranger. This morning was only a makeshift at best. The table linen was at the bottom of a trunk, and she had spread newspapers on the table. But she got out a few pieces of old china, that had been in her mother's family nobody knew how many years, which the doctor noticed and admired, and altogether they had a merry breakfast of it.

"Now," said the doctor, pushing his chair back and declaring that he had made a heartier breakfast than he had enjoyed for months; "I propose that we start out on a tour of discovery. I confess that I, for one, am very curious to know just what there is on the ranch. Why, what is this! You have a dog?"

For a huge shadow had darkened the door, and there stood the great Newfoundland, a little refreshed by his dinner of the night before, but still gaunt and weak.

"We found him in the house," explained Martin.

"In the house?" repeated the doctor, looking puzzled. "Was there any sign of anything else — of any human being — about?"

"No, sir," replied Ned. "It looks to me as if the poor fellow had been here a long time. He is very lame; he has a bad leg. There was a path worn down to the water that I think he must have made. The weeds came together above. We could n't use it till we cut them away."

"The man who used to live here had a dog like this, a large Newfoundland puppy," said the doctor reflectively. "I wonder if he could have left him here, and the dog survived all these years.

He was a brutal fellow,— the man. Come here, old fellow, and let me see your leg."

The dog labored across the floor and sat down at Dr. John's feet. The doctor examined the injured member.

"That was done by a blow or a kick," he said.

"Oh, how cruel!" cried Hope. "And he left the dog here to suffer and starve. What could he have lived on?"

"I don't know. Fish from the stream, perhaps. I have heard of animals changing their nature in such cases, and turning graminivorous. He certainly would have proved up his title to the ranch if a dog could do it. He is in a sorry condition for hunting. I might help the leg even now, poor fellow, but it will hurt. Shall I do it?"

There was something almost human in the dog's low whine, the appeal of his honest eyes.

"Very well, sir. Take firm hold up here, Ned. Don't let the dog stir if you can help it."

Dr. John took hold of the lower portion of the injured leg, and pulled with great force upon it. The stiffened cords and muscles gave way, there was a dull crunch of bones, and the joint settled back into place.

"Now for splints and bandages," said the doctor. "Brave old fellow! He is a regular 'Old Dog Tray,' and we must call him so. It will never be a pretty leg again, but with good care he can walk more comfortably after this. Now I have an hour more to spare, and we must spend it looking around."

The children started up eagerly, and together they went out of the front door, and standing for a moment at the edge of the natural terrace whereon the house stood, looked down upon The Brook and off across the country.

Hope gave an exclamation of delight. The hills approached so closely to them, on either side, that they seemed to be looking through a mountainous gateway. The rich browns of the bare rocks and faded yellows of the dried grasses struck sharply against the moist greens of the low-lying valley, with its extensive orchards and vineyards. The Brook, arched with living green in the foreground, wound like a silver ribbon through the valley, until it became merged in a broader sheet of silver in the distance, which they knew to be the beautiful Bay of San Francisco, the noblest harbor in the world. The purple hills of the peninsula bounded the horizon.

"Look off there to the left, boys," said the doctor.

They looked in the direction which he indicated, and saw some rows of stunted trees struggling above the tall weeds.

"An orchard!" cried both boys in a breath.

It was an orchard, but such a starved and blighted one that it seemed a mere caricature of the thriving growths in the valley below. They threaded their way to it with difficulty. There were twenty rows of trees, originally numbering about twenty trees to the row, but many had died in infancy and decayed to the ground, while others had fallen a prey to burrowing rodents or insect pests, and still stood upright, their leafless branches overgrown with lichens.

"What puzzles me," said Dr. John, looking about him, "is the fact that Hank Jones, the lazy fellow who took up this claim, should have had sufficient enterprise to plant out even this mongrel collection of trees."

"I have it!" he exclaimed, a moment later. "The man was a great glutton; lazy people invariably are. Whenever he ate a peach or plum or any other kind of fruit, and he was convenient to the spot, he planted the pit or seed. This orchard represents his gourmandizing at different periods during the year he lived up here. He ate a couple of dozen apricots at a sitting one day, and this row of apricot trees — half are living and half of them are dead — was the result. Then he ate a handful of cherries, and planted the pits over there. At some time or other, he got hold of a mixed lot of plums and peaches, and that gives us this mixed row. Only one thing disputes my theory: how he ever managed to deny himself that walnut and those almonds, I cannot understand."

They all laughed gleefully, and a magical echo answered from the hills.

"What makes the ground so hard?" asked Ned, striking his heel against the earth, which gave back a ringing, flinty sound.

"The same cause that makes the trees so stunted and the fruit so worthless, — lack of cultivation," was the reply. "The ground has been allowed to bake after the rains, and the weeds have sapped most of the moisture and the vitality from it. If it had been properly cultivated the weeds would have been kept down, and the crumbly top soil would have condensed moisture from the atmosphere, instead of perpetually giving to it. If these trees were mine, boys, I am not sure whether I should try to make them of some account, or root them up and plant new in their place."

They were walking toward the house again, and for the first time they noticed that Hope was laboring under happy excitement.

"Oh, boys! And Dr. John! Now you must come and see what I have found," she cried.

She had run on ahead, and was leading the way toward the hills behind the house. When she had gone a little distance she stopped, and beckoned them to come.

There was a spring of crystal pure water, a great, bowl-shaped hollow in the rocks, the overflow from which formed a tiny brooklet, that gurgled over the ground for a short distance and then, not having sufficient force or volume to find its way to The Brook, soon disappeared from sight. Beside it a wild rose was pink with bloom. But it was not this to which the young girl was pointing, with eyes that sparkled, and her mouth wreathed in a happy smile. Directly in the path of the spring's overflow there stood a large orange-tree. Untouched by the beauty-destroying hand of the horticulturist, it had attained a noble growth, and from crown to root its dense foliage formed a rich setting for the wealth of yellow-green and golden fruit that hung upon it. It was evidently a seedling which had come into bearing a couple of years before, for the largest of its fruit, when subjected to examination, showed a sponge-like rind an inch thick, with a partially dried pulp in the centre, while the second-sized oranges were also distinguished by heavy rinds, but were still sweet and juicy.

As they came down from the spring, Ned, who had been very silent during the latter part of their walk, looked troubled and dejected. They stopped a moment to look at an old building in the rear of the house. It was built of hewn logs, mortised together at the corners, and provided with a stout roof of similar construction, which had been plastered with clay. It had no window or opening of any kind, save a small, clumsy door, that fastened with a heavy hasp and staple. A huge padlock hung from the latter.

"What an odd place!" exclaimed Martin.

"A regular old-fashioned smokehouse, such as you will find everywhere throughout the South," commented the doctor.

The children looked at it curiously for a moment, and then passed it by, little foreseeing the important part it was to play in an exciting episode of the years to come.

As they neared the house, Ned laid his hand on the doctor's arm.

"Dr. John, may I speak to you for one minute alone?" he asked.

"Certainly, Ned," replied the doctor, wondering what could have brought the look of trouble and perplexity to the young fellow's face.

They moved off in the direction of the orchard, where Ned took his stand with folded arms, and remained for a moment silent with embarrassment.

"Out with it!" commanded Dr. John.

"Why, you see, it came over me down here in the orchard. You talked about pruning, and thinning, and cultivating. I have n't the slightest idea what any of them mean. Dr. John, I've come out here to make a living as a farmer, and I don't know the first thing about farming."

Ned was a little exasperated to see the doctor's eyes twinkle, his mouth twitch, and finally to behold him convulsed with laughter.

"It may seem very funny to you, Dr. John," said the boy sadly, "but it's no laughing matter to me, if I'm going to make a failure of it."

"It's not that, Ned,— not that," laughed the doctor. "But to think that a boy of your age should make the discovery so soon. There are dozens of men in the valley who would give thousands of dollars to have found that very thing out in time. The trouble is that they always start in thinking that they *do* know, you see. Don't worry, my boy. You're safe."

"But I've got to learn somehow or other," insisted Ned. "I don't even know what tools and implements to buy, or what to plant."

"The easiest thing in the world to find out. Go to some one who has had experience and has made a practical success. Go to Mr. Abbott, our nurseryman, the one who wanted to negotiate for your calf. Tell him just how much money you've got, and ask his advice about expending it."

Ned's heart was very much lightened as they returned to the house, where Martin seized the opportunity for himself and accosted Dr. John.

"Haven't you any wife or children?"

Like most boys of his age, he always had a question on the tip of his tongue.

Neither of the three ever forgot the reply.

A change swept over the doctor's face, making it look gray and old, all in an instant.

"I had," he said hoarsely. "But it's like your land here. It's an 'abandoned claim.' I never 'proved up.'"

CHAPTER X.

A BUSY DAY.

A WEEK later Ned went down to Oakland and entered the land in due form. When he came back he got his horse from Dr. John's stable, and returned home by the hill road, stopping at the Abbott nursery on the way.

The hours he spent with the old man were a liberal education in fruit farming. Mr. Abbott helped him to lay out his purchasing fund to the best advantage, aiding him to economize by turning over to him some old implements cast aside on his own place to make room for newer patents, but which were still in good condition. He also solved one of their perplexities by offering them the use of a fallow cow, in return for her pasturage, until their own animal should be old enough to supply them with milk. He advised him to put the upper portion of his level land into early peas, in order to get returns on a winter's crop.

"How many rows of peas, two hundred feet long, do you think you and your brother could plant, and keep well hoed, between now and next February?" asked the old gentleman.

"About three hundred," returned Ned, after a little reflection.

"Then try a hundred and fifty. That will be one half. With some boys I should have advised only one third or one fourth, but I think you have a fair degree of prudence, and would not be likely to estimate your strength or capability at more than double their worth."

Despite Ned's shy protestations, Mr. Abbott took him at noon to a cozy little dining-room, where a bountiful meal was spread, and where he made the acquaintance of a beautiful old lady, as bright and quaint in her way as Mr. Abbott was in his. At the table all business topics were dropped, and while host and hostess showed a gentle solicitude for the comfort of their young guest, the conversation ran on larger themes, and Ned found himself listening to an intelligent, broad-minded discussion of the great world's affairs, which lifted him into a new plane of thought and feeling. Inexperienced as he was in many ways, intuition taught him that the engravings on the wall, the books distributed about, were products of the world's master minds, and made a fit setting for these two gentle and cultured old people, the types of many more, distributed throughout town and country, who are insensibly moulding the destiny of California.

The road Ned took on his way over the hills followed the edge of the valley, along the line of the foothills, which were everywhere fringed with beautiful farms, the vineyards and grain fields in some instances extending far up the hill slopes.

At length his course turned directly toward the

Range, following the bank of a deep ravine, along whose bed a tiny mountain stream glanced and sparkled. Steep as the road was in places, it was as finely macadamized as the drives in Golden Gate Park. It soon passed the first line of hills, but Ned found that what had from the valley looked like a single row of peaks was in reality but one of an extensive system.

The road dipped into slight depressions, only to rise again and again to bleaker heights. In many of these sheltered mountain benches little farm-houses were standing, and now and then a goodly patch of vineyard or a bit of thriving orchard bore witness to the enterprise of the settlers, and stood as a smiling prediction of the future; but oftener the heights were barren and desolate, and the ground was honeycombed by ground squirrels, thousands of which stood like mimic sentinels before the entrances to their underground abodes. Once a coyote came out upon a bleak and wind-swept ledge, and grimly surveyed the boy. At length the summit of the range was reached, and the road began to descend, by easy gradations, to the level of the valley beyond.

It was a long and toilsome journey, but it afforded the boy what he most needed: time to think.

The events of the past few weeks had crowded so closely upon each other that he had been forced to act promptly, and frequently with little deliberation. For the first time in his life, he began to forecast the future, and prepared himself to face the inevitable disappointments that must come in the new life. He foresaw that he would often be tired and discouraged, and that his burden of responsibility would press heavily upon him. He knew that he should miss the stimulus of school life, the sharp competition, the pleasures of companionship with other boys of his age; he knew that Martin, two years younger than he, younger still by force of natural temperament, would often weary and irritate him. Martin did not like work. He was heedless, impracticable, visionary. Yet this was the sort of life to school him into regular and industrious habits, — if only Martin could be schooled.

And Hope. Gentle little Hope! It would be a lonely life for her, and a wearing one. What if she should break down and fade out of life, as their mother had done? How vigilantly they must watch to spare her undue labor; what zealous guard must he keep over his own anxieties, to prevent her life from being overcast by them!

Following the directions of some people he met, he turned into an old road which soon dwindled into a mere bridle path. After following this for a mile or more, the boy suddenly stopped short, and gave an exclamation of surprise.

A turn in the path brought into sight a spectacle so at variance with all the landscape that for a moment he was tempted to rub his eyes, and question whether he were not dreaming.

All of the ranches he had hitherto seen bore

some evidences of thrift and comfort. Even the swarthy little Portuguese children, short of skirt and bare of limb, were tidily clad and bore themselves with an air of self-respecting reserve, as if the tiniest among them had some part in the great plan of life, if only to oil the wheels that other people made go round.

Before him was a dilapidated shanty, looking more as if it belonged to the dingiest portion of Tar Flat in San Francisco than to pure, vitalizing country air. Broken window-panes were stuffed with gunny-sacks and castaway clothing. Unpainted and decaying, the battens that originally covered the seams between the boards had been splintered off in places, revealing wide cracks, through which an inquisitive eye might have searched the whole interior. There was no attempt at a garden, front or rear, save one small patch, a few rods from the house, where some sickly-looking cabbage plants strained upwards for a glimpse of light, inclosed by a miniature rail fence. A great boy sat astride the upper rail, gun in hand, his eyes intently fixed upon some object invisible to Ned, while a smaller boy crouched a little distance away.

In the doorway of the shanty there sat a slatternly woman, a soiled gingham sunbonnet pushed back from her forehead, and a clay pipe between her lips. Around her sprawled several more children of the same type, their hair unkempt, their faces obscured with dirt.

"Good-afternoon, ma'am," said Ned politely.

"Aft'noon," responded the woman indifferently, without removing the pipe from her mouth, while her hand, from force of habit, sought the front of her dress waist and endeavored to supply the lack of buttons.

"Can you tell me the way to the McCrary ranch?" asked Ned.

The woman took the pipe from her mouth, and eyed him with a look of cunning suspicion.

"Be yees afther the road tax?" she asked sharply.

"Oh, no, indeed," answered Ned, smiling.

"Ner the poll tax?"

"No, ma'am."

"An yees ain't sint by the assissor?"

"Why, no, ma'am. I'm quite a stranger here. We have taken up the claim down opposite Dr. John's."

The woman's face relaxed as if by magic. A look of genuine kindliness came into her homely face.

"Wan of thim pore boys! Come in an' set yersilf down, an' have a glass of milk. Yees must be clane tired out, wid ridin' so far."

"Oh, no, I thank you," returned Ned, to whom the prospect of the glass of milk did not appear half as attractive as it might have, if her hands and surroundings had been cleaner, and there had been no pipe. "To tell the truth, I'm in quite a hurry to reach home before sundown. I wanted to see about some chickens. Mr. Abbott said he thought you might have some laying hens to sell."

"Plinty av thim. The thrubble ud be the catchin' av thim. They're all over the ranch. Lay off in the chap'ral iverywhere. Jist natrally run wild!"

"Can I see — Mike?" asked Ned, somewhat abashed at this unpromising outlook.

"'S over there," grunted the woman, who had settled back to her pipe and was lazily puffing away.

She pointed in the direction of the cabbage patch. Ned tied his horse to a maimed oak-tree near the door, a considerable portion of which had been hacked away for the purpose of firewood, and walked quietly toward the two boys. As he was almost upon them the younger put up his hand in warning, but it was too late.

"Now you've done it!" he cried, addressing Ned.

"Done what?" demanded Ned, in astonishment.

"Oh, nothing," replied the elder boy, lifting his gun to his shoulder with a disappointed air, then rising and stretching out his long limbs, lifting a torn straw hat from his head and thereby revealing a good-natured and somewhat comely face, with curling, reddish hair, and frank blue eyes.

"It's nothing," he explained, in amiable resignation, albeit there was a touch of irony in his tone, "*only* I'd been after that gopher all day yisterday an' since sun-up this morning, an' — I jist had him! Another second, sir, an' I'd 'a' popped him over!"

"What had he done?" asked Ned.

"Done? He was a gopher. You bet he'll do enough. He's got his eye on those cabbages."

Ned thought to himself that if some one else would have an eye to the cabbages, the cabbages would be none the worse for it. The poor plants were wretched starvelings, choked out by tall weeds that pressed upon them from every side. He could not resist reaching over the rude fence and freeing one of the poor plants from the enemies that encompassed it. Mike McCrary watched the action in dumb surprise.

"I wanted to see you about some chickens," explained Ned pleasantly; "though now that I have spoiled your sport, I don't know that you will want to accommodate me. I'd like to get a dozen laying hens."

"What'll you give?" asked Mike McCrary.

"Would five dollars be enough?"

Mike scowled reflectively.

"It's a sight of trouble to chase 'em through the chap'ral, or hunt 'em up in the trees at night. But I'm out o' caps an' powder. Blissed if I don't do it! When you want 'em? Come after 'em yersilf?"

"If you say so," returned Ned seriously. "We're your new neighbors. We've taken up the claim down by The Brook."

"No! One of thim lunatics? Let me have a good squint at yer," ejaculated Mike, with a look of mingled contempt and humor.

Ignorant of his meaning, Ned returned his gaze with serious dignity.

"What possessed yer, anyhow?" pursued Mike. "They say yer goin' to farm it. Don't yer know farmin' means — work?"

He pronounced the last word in a tone expressive of such horror and aversion that Ned laughed outright.

"Work?" he said. "Why, that's just what we came up here for. The more the better. I like work."

Mike McCrary had doubtless heard the philosophy of work preached more than once in his life, but this was the first time he had heard it proclaimed with honest sincerity by one of his own age, who turned theory into practice.

"Jiminy!" was all he said.

He accompanied Ned to the bluff, to point out to him the steep and narrow trail that would take him home.

"I'll bring down the chickens myself," he said awkwardly, as they parted. "I'd like to have a good look at you fellers that like work!"

CHAPTER XI.

A HOME AND THREE PATRIOTS.

As he came in sight of the low cottage, nestling in the hollow of the hills, Ned felt a sensation he had never known before. For the first time he understood a sentence he had once heard fall from the lips of an orator of national repute.

"*The home makes the patriot. No man ever shouldered a musket in defense of a boarding-house.*"

"Or a tenement house either," thought the boy. The shabby little dwelling toward which he was now going was no longer mean or shabby in his eyes. It was exalted by the glory of possession. He did not see the battered walls, the cracked windows, the clumsy doors. No palace, to which other people held the title-deeds, could be half so beautiful to him.

Hope ran out to meet him when she saw him coming. She led him to the front door, and laughed aloud in delight at his exclamation of pleasure and surprise. The large room had been thoroughly cleaned, and the redwood boards with which it was ceiled lent a rich and effective background for the knickknacks, bunches of dried grasses, and richly tinted leaves that were arranged upon the walls. Halfway up the chimney breast, Martin had suspended some hanging shelves of redwood that they had brought with them, and upon these stood a glass filled with pink roses, whose perfume filled the room. The only carpet they had brought with them, a crimson ingrain, was tacked in the centre of the room. Hope had festooned some dotted Swiss muslin above the windows, catching it up with cypress boughs, while the Madras curtains that had hung at her own window were strung across one corner of the room, to shut the boys' bed off from sight. A little stand covered with books, the crimson-covered lounge, and a couple of chairs completed the furniture of the room; but, bare as it was, it had an air of comfort and of cheer, often lacking in elegantly furnished parlors.

In Hope's own little room adjoining, after much thoughtful consideration, they had put the pretty set of bedroom furniture that had been their parents', and with which they could not bear to part. Hope's own little bed was dislocated and stood up in one corner of the room.

The stuffy, untidy kitchen was stuffy and untidy no longer. The walks had been brushed down, the floor scrubbed, and all the unpleasant reminders of former occupancy removed. Nails had been driven along the walls, and various shining utensils hung upon them, while at one side were a couple of neat shelves, the product of Martin's genius. It was a little crowded, it is true, and there was no room for the kitchen safe they had brought, which had been placed outside the door.

Ned therefore resolved to contrive a pantry for the little housewife's comfort. With Dr. John's coöperation, he procured the necessary lumber, and built a rough but airy and water-tight addition to the kitchen, placing it in the angle between the shed and the main portion of the house, where it was only necessary to build two walls, a floor, and a roof, to make the small room complete. When he had finished the pantry he moved in the meal-chest, and arranged all the utensils and materials commonly used in cooking, so that the young cook could prepare a dish for the oven without taking unnecessary steps.

Hope watched these arrangements with admiring surprise.

"Women and girls can *do* things pretty well, but I believe it takes men and boys to plan for them," she said.

While Ned was at work on the pantry, Martin completed a rough chicken-house which they had both framed together. These tasks completed, the serious work of the season commenced.

"Upon my word, boys, this begins to look home-like," said Dr. John, coming up by The Brook path a few weeks later.

The tall growth of weeds extending from the house to the water had been cleared away, leaving only a short, dry stubble, that would readily yield to the plough when the ground should be soaked by rain. The broken panes of glass had been replaced, and the roses that enwreathed the cottage had been neatly trimmed, while some slips that Hope brought from the city were thriving in the true "leaf mould," so dear to the professional florist.

"The place begins to look as if it belonged to somebody," asserted the doctor. "You ought to christen it."

"I think it should be Home Ranch," said a gentle voice, and Hope stood beside them.

So Home Ranch it became from that day, and if anything could have made the little nook dearer to its occupants, it would have been because it bore this suggestive name.

"We shall have rain soon," said Dr. John. "Better get in all your supplies, boys, and make ready for a siege."

"Oh, this is only a fog," said Martin.

"When a fog broods over the earth day after day, at this time of year, it generally means business," said the doctor pleasantly, for it was late in October. "Look off across the valley, and see how distinct and near at hand appear the church spires of that little village six miles away. This clarified atmosphere means rain."

The doctor was right, and by nightfall a light rain was falling. Softly and steadily it fell,— "Heaven-sent dew," as Ned called it; and the parched earth absorbed it greedily, while all vegetation, including, alas! even the weeds, seemed to revive beneath it.

On the morning of the third day they awoke to find the land bathed in sunshine. Ned gave his sleeping brother a vigorous shake.

"Get up, Martin. We must plough to-day."

Do you know what is meant by virgin soil? It means soil that has been garnering up its wealth from time immemorial; soil that has never been robbed or impoverished by the hand of man. Since the world began, every blade that has burst its sheath, every leaf and flower that have unfolded, has returned again to Mother Earth, to gladden and enrich her. Scoop up a handful of it: no hard crusts or heavy clods here; it crumbles at the touch. Press it with your foot: it yields like a sponge, but never packs. Smell of it: it has an invigorating perfume. There is a suggestion of life and of life-giving power in its very color, that warm, purplish tinge, fading to amethyst in the sunlight.

In such soil the boys had their first experience in driving the plough, and for a time the delight intoxicated them; but it was not long before their untried muscles called for a rest. Ned was too plucky to abandon work altogether, and he insisted upon harrowing the patch they had ploughed, and then running their lines and dropping the peas in the small furrows, covering them with the hoe as fast as a line was finished.

It is very simple and easy in the telling; but it

took both of the boys until sundown to plough and harrow less than a quarter of an acre of ground, and then to plant it in peas. They were so tired and stiff when they were through that it was hard to attend to their accustomed chores before going to bed; but sleep, the true elixir of life, restored them, and they awoke the next morning with renewed strength.

"I'm so tired and sore, I'd like to lie down and not get up again for a month," groaned Martin, a couple of weeks later, when the peas were all in.

Weary as they were, they dared not rest. They had to lay in a winter's store of firewood, and the ground in the old orchard needed to be ploughed. Meanwhile, the peas came up and grew apace; but the weeds, too, answered the muster call, and it became necessary to wage war upon them.

The young people found, to their delight, that the early rains only served to swell the volume and increase the current of The Brook for a few days, after which the stream subsided, and was easily crossed with the raft. The boys came and went freely between Home Ranch and the village, but little Hope never dared trust herself to the raft a second time.

CHAPTER XII.

A MYSTERIOUS JOURNEY.

"Martin, don't you want to take a ride with me to-morrow?" asked Dr. John one day early in December.

"I'll be very glad to, sir," and the boy's eyes sparkled with anticipation.

"Very well," said Dr. John, "be on hand early in the morning, say seven o'clock, and prepare to be away the whole forenoon."

"Is it somebody very sick, or far away?"

"Eh? Oh, yes. A good ways off," replied the doctor, who seemed to be unaccountedly embarrassed by the simple question.

Martin had read several stories of detective experience, and, like many boys of his age, had conceived the idea that he would have great talent for the profession. He had determined to cultivate a habit of perpetual watchfulness in every-day life, and to permit no suspicious detail to escape him.

He did not wish to believe evil of a man who had proved himself in so many ways their faithful and unselfish friend, yet he had never been able to wholly dismiss from his mind the schoolmaster's dark and significant allusion. Dr. John's singular hesitation and confusion impressed the boy, and he looked forward to the morrow with a curiosity not unmixed with dread.

Martin was on hand bright and early the next morning, as he had promised. The doctor drove directly to the station, and then turned northward on a road that ran parallel with the railroad track over which they had come from the city. Martin thought the doctor must be going to the next village, but when the next village and the next were passed, he began to see that Dr. John was aiming for some distant town.

He thought he understood when they approached the outskirts of Oakland. So the doctor's patient lived there, and must be some rich person to afford to call a physician from such a distance. But why should Dr. John make such a mystery about it? Why should he be so strangely morose, scarcely heeding the boy's innocent questions, called forth by sights along their route, until the young fellow subsided into a hurt silence? Why should he drive directly into the heart of the city, and draw up on a business street, a few doors away from one of the large banks?

"Now, Martin," he said, producing a small bag of specie, "I want you to do a little business for me. You see that bank over there?"

"Yes, sir."

"Take this money and say that Richard Roe, or George Smith, or anybody you please, so that it is not my name, deposits it. Ask for a draft made out in the name of E. F. Sherwood, of Philadelphia. Be very careful about that last name. Better write it down. Have you a bit of paper and a pencil? Here, take mine."

Martin wrote the name with care, and awaited further instructions.

"Be sure not to have anything to say to any one, aside from what I have told you. If they ask you anything more, tell them you don't know. Get out again as soon as you can, and bring the draft to me."

With a sinking heart Martin took the bag in his hands. At last he understood the meaning of the mysterious journey. The doctor was launched in a career of crime, and he, Martin, was to be his accomplice. For one moment the boy had a wild thought of refusing to be involved in any such villainous scheme, but he looked in the doctor's eye, and felt himself under its power.

The bag was heavier than it looked. It contained considerably more money than he had ever before handled; yet he could feel no pride in touching it, and he went up the steps of the building with his head hanging and shame in his heart.

Martin had no experience of banking laws, and was quite in the dark as to the precise relation of the money to the paper he was to get; but he knew enough of life to be fully aware that when a man acts in secret, it is because he has something disgraceful to conceal.

He looked so downcast and guilty when he presented himself at the desk of the receiving teller that the official regarded him with rank suspicion, and examined the coins minutely, to assure himself they were not counterfeit. Martin would not have been surprised at any moment to find himself taken into legal custody, and marched off to the city prison.

He was greatly relieved when he got safely back to Dr. John, and handed him the paper. Dr. John, too, was manifestly lighter of heart, and spoke up quite like his usual self : —

"Now I want to drive around to the post-office, and stop there a moment, and then we will go home."

"But your patient, doctor, — the sick person you came all this way to see!"

"Oh, I think the sick person will get along very well to-day," answered the doctor shamelessly.

At the post-office Martin observed that the doctor took from his pocket an envelope, bearing an address printed with a typewriter, inclosed the draft, and mailed it in the usual way.

On the way home Martin's head was in a whirl. Puzzle as he might, he could not arrive at any theory that would account for the peculiar facts. Yet there was no question as to the doctor's guilt. The doctor himself tacitly admitted it when they reached their starting-point, and drove into the shadows of his home.

"Martin," he said, "you are a boy who can keep a secret, are you not?"

"Yes, sir," returned Martin staunchly.

"I thought so. I shall trust you never to say anything about our ride this morning, or the errand you did for me."

"I promise, honor bright," said poor Martin, but it was with a heavy heart.

CHAPTER XIII.

WINTER ON A CALIFORNIA RANCH.

THANKSGIVING and Christmas passed with little observance at Home Ranch. The children's hearts were yet too sore with recent sorrow for them to take thought of any merry-making. On Christmas Day Ned went down to the city alone to see their father, bearing such simple remembrances as they were able to send; but the lad met with a rebuff from one of the physicians at the hospital, who fancied that he saw in the father's natural emotion at seeing one of the children from whom he had been so long separated, the tokens of an excitement that might be injurious to his patient.

The day after New Year's, Hope sat on a low block outside of the kitchen door, patiently turning a crank attached to a large wooden contrivance, shaped very much like an ancient Pompeiian jug. She was listening intently to the sound of something splashing about inside.

Hope's churning was a profound and mysterious rite, and the boys were not allowed to approach or to speak to her during the process, for she had a theory that if she was interrupted for a moment the butter would " go back," and the cream relapse into its original liquid state.

The boys' milking, as well as Hope's butter-making, had been studied up from a little agricultural manual that Ned had picked up at a second-hand bookstand, before they left the city.

This treatise, written by an English gentleman-farmer and printed some fifty years before, dealt with the subject in a tone of dignified condescension, and abounded in high-sounding phrases and digressions from the text, which would delight our agricultural editors of to-day. The chapter devoted to the milch cow began as follows : —

"The genus *bos*, commonly called *neat*, and sometimes *black cattle*, stands at the head of our domestic animals destined for the use and food of man, and more especially for that precious alimentary production, MILK, of such importance in rearing our children and adapted to such a variety of other family purposes. For a constant supply of this invaluable resource, we depend on the female of this race, the harmless and docile cow, which is compelled to produce and part with that secretion, intended by nature for the support of her own progeny."

As Hope heard the watery swash which announced that the butter had "come," she turned with an expression of dismay to a little clock hanging in the kitchen.

"Oh, dear!" she said aloud. "Only seven minutes again."

"And who is it bewailing seven minutes lost?" called out a cheery voice, and Dr. John came around the corner of the house.

"It isn't exactly seven minutes lost, doctor,"

replied Hope seriously; "but I can't seem to keep the butter back till the proper time."

"And, pray, what is the proper time?" asked the doctor mystified.

"The time in the book," explained Hope, pointing to the book lying open beside the churn. Dr. John took it up and read the paragraph to which she pointed:—

"' Butter which comes too quickly is not likely to be good, nor ought any to come, indeed, under an hour's labour.' Why, what sort of a book is this?" demanded the doctor, turning over the leaves. "Listen to this advice: ' It is recommended to confine the hinder legs of a cow, whilst milking, as well as the head, the former of which is most securely effected by two stumps of wood fixed in the ground, to which the hinder legs may be strapped.' I should like to see a California cow submit to such an indignity."

"She does n't submit. She acts awfully. She kicks, and lashes her tail, and tumbles over, and holds back her milk, and tries to hook. Ned has an awful time whenever he milks her," explained Hope.

"So Ned is trying it?" cried Dr. John, making a severe effort to compose his face, but unable to subdue the merry twinkle in his eye. "I shall have to tell the boys not to go by all the advice they find in books. And don't worry about the butter if it chooses to come at the first turn of the crank. But what has this to do with cows?" and looking further on, in the same chapter, the doctor read as follows: —

"'In years past I had a fine cat, which we named Bonaparte, and which we suffered to retain that splendid name, until his godfather became an apostate and a tyrant.' Why, Ned," he said, as the boy came in, "this book is a regular curiosity: worth its weight in gold to some of our bibliomaniacs. But don't try to farm by it."

"I don't intend to any longer," answered Ned. "We have something better now. Mr. Roberts has sent us a complete set of the —— Encyclopædia."

"Indeed," exclaimed Dr. John, his eyes brightening. "That is a gift worth having. I came over intending to make a little contribution to your reading matter myself. I have a morning and an evening paper daily, an illustrated weekly or so, and several magazines every month. Suppose I send over to you all that has accumulated at the end of every week. Of course they won't be very fresh, but they will help you to keep up with the world's news."

"It will be a great treat," said Ned heartily. "I'm not sure but it will be much better for us not to have them oftener. Reading is such a temptation. It would be hard to go about our work, with a fresh newspaper unread."

Ned was thinking of Martin rather than himself. The doctor's next question brought back to him the unhappy memory of his recent experience.

"How is your father, Ned? I understand you have been down to see him."

"About the same, sir, I should judge. I don't know when any of us will see him again. They don't want us to come there."

"Don't want you to come?" repeated Dr. John, in amazement.

"No, sir. The doctor there thinks it does him harm, — excites him. We hoped to go down more, after a while. It must be so tiresome for him, lying there day after day, seeing nobody that really cares for him."

Dr. John said nothing by way of comment, but he paced up and down, as he was in the habit of doing when deeply stirred, with his lips firmly set and a stern look on his face. At length he stopped short, with an air of cheerful determination.

"I see just one way out of it," he said. "These hospital authorities are very arbitrary sometimes, and it is not wise to defy them. But I know a man — I have a friend who will go to see your father every week, and carry any messages you may like to send, and bring us reports of his condition."

"We could n't ask for anything better," declared Ned, and Martin's look of relief and Hope's bright eyes confirmed his assertion.

After Dr. John left, they remembered that this was the first time they had seen him since the holidays. They wondered if he had been away, and how he had spent the time. Had they but known it, the question was one that had for many years puzzled the people of the valley. Genial as the doctor was in his relations with his patients, he always declined the invitations that were pressed upon him at this period of the year, and on Christmas Day he always shut himself up in his house, never leaving it unless in obedience to some urgent professional summons.

It was about this time that Dr. John took to church-going. He had never been a very zealous attendant at divine service before, having quite outraged the feelings of the more conservative in the community, by spending the hours that others passed in the house of worship at the bedside of sick children, showing them pictures, telling them stories, and inventing all manner of amusements for them. Now he became a steady church-goer, and rose in public estimation accordingly, although he did not patronize local theology, but went off on the early Sunday morning train, presumably to listen to the gospel as expounded by some brilliant Oakland or San Francisco divine.

CHAPTER XIV.

THE ROPE EXPRESS.

DECEMBER had been an open and pleasant month, made up of warm and sunshiny days, interspersed with a few light showers. The California climate, so extravagantly extolled by many, so unjustly denounced by a few, is little understood even by those who have lived under it the better portion of their lives.

It is common to hear old Californians boastfully declare that the State has no seasons, whereas each month brings its varying changes as surely as the year comes round. In the city the skillful gardener's artifice does much to smooth away these differences and to make all months alike; but those who live in the country know that California has her seasons, clear cut and well defined as those of New England, the distinction being that while New England boasts of four, the Golden State has but three, and two of these, spring and fall, are robbed of much their harshness, their poetry and beauty alone being preserved.

January is a month of compromise between fall and spring. It is sure to bring many chilly, wet, and disagreeable days. Even at Home Ranch there were nights when the mercury hovered about the freezing point, and once it dropped a single degree below, but Hope's delicate plants were uninjured, while the hardy peas seemed to grow and thrive the better.

In the intervals between the rains, the boys laid out the new orchard they meant to plant, and dug holes for the young trees. Meanwhile, the "state of siege" which the doctor had predicted came upon them with the beginning of the new year. After a week or so of rainy weather the stream became so swollen that it spread out over the lowlands along its banks, snatching the raft from its moorings and sweeping it down the stream. Thereafter they were completely cut off from intercourse with all the rest of the world, and it was only human for the three children to feel a little lonely, and to look forward yearningly to the time when they could have communication with their friends again.

With the beginning of February, spring burst suddenly upon them. The almond trees in the orchard, which had retained their fresh green foliage until Christmas, expanded into a radiance of bloom.

"Martin," said Ned solemnly, "if we are going to prune those trees, as the doctor and Mr. Abbott advised us, we mustn't lose another day."

"All right," said Martin. "But what are we to do the pruning with?"

True enough. They had neglected to provide themselves with pruning shears, knife, or saw.

"We'll just have to take the compass saw from our tool chest, and the large handsaw, and make our jackknives do the rest."

So the two set to work, making up in energy what they lacked in skill and experience.

"I'll tell you what I mean to do, if our peas come out well, as they give every promise of doing," announced Ned one day, as he lopped off a huge peach limb and flung it upon a pile of brush. "I'm going to get some grape-vines, and set them out in the same patch, when we tear up the pea-vines. The ground is already cultivated, and cuttings are only three dollars a thousand. We can plant as many as we have time to put in before April is over."

"Good!" approved Martin. "I should like to have a vineyard of our own. I always did like grapes, and grape pies, and grape jelly — Why, Ned! what's the matter?"

Ned had suspended his work, and sat weakly down on a heap of brush, gazing moodily before him.

"The peas," he explained. "Oh, Martin! why didn't we think of it before? Why didn't anybody think of it for us?"

"The peas?" repeated Martin. "What's the matter with the peas? I'm sure there's a splendid crop, Ned. I was looking at them this morning. They'll be ready for market by the end of this month."

"How are we going to get them to market?"

Martin came down out of the apricot-tree, into which he had climbed, and joined his brother on the brush heap.

"Make a new raft?" he suggested.

"And try to pole it a hundred feet across that boiling torrent!" answered Ned disdainfully. "A boat couldn't live in it."

"Then there's no way but to go round by the hill road."

"What? Risk our horses' necks and our own, by climbing up that slippery trail? Let down a rope and grappling iron for the peas after getting ourselves up; then crawl around the hills for miles, carrying a single sack of peas to the station? Oh, a fine condition they would be in, by the time they got there," observed Ned ironically. "I don't see any way out of it, unless the doctor can help us; but how we can even remind him of the plight we're in is more than I can see."

Dr. John was not one of the sort of people who need reminding. For days he had been thinking of the young people's situation, and trying to devise some means of escape from it.

That very afternoon they heard a faint halloo above the roaring of the waters, and running down to the bank of the stream, found Dr. John standing on the other side, with a coil of rope beside him, and what looked like a large bow and arrow in his hand.

He pointed to a tall sycamore on their side of The Brook, taking aim high up among the branches.

As he let the arrow fly, a slender cord trailed through the air in its wake. The arrow fled through the sycamore, but the cord became tangled in the boughs and arrested its progress. They saw it dangling there.

The doctor waved his hand in the direction of the arrow, and began to pay out string. Ned obeyed the hint, and climbed the tree, drawing in the cord. A length of heavy twine followed the cord, and to this was attached some stout manilla rope, which brought with it a solid iron pulley, such as is ordinarily attached to hoisting tackle. Martin cried out in delight, as he saw the doctor's purpose. Taking advantage of two great sycamores, which stood on opposite sides of the stream, he was rigging up a cord and pulley for conveying weights across, as cables are sometimes attached to wrecked vessels, to convey passengers and valuables ashore.

Soon it became Ned's turn to send back the cord, that the rope might be returned to the other side. With a boy's ready ingenuity he prepared a rude bow, and, after a little bungling archery, sent the arrow successfully across.

The pulleys were soon secured to the old sycamores, and the line was in working order.

Martin, who had quite expected to see Dr. John himself climb into a great hamper and make the trip across, and who was secretly entertaining great schemes of aerial travel for his own amusement, was somewhat disappointed to see a small, covered basket secured to the rope and sent across. When opened, it proved to be full of papers and magazines, with a note to Hope on top. On the outside of this was a penciled inquiry addressed to the boys:—

"How soon will your peas be ready for market?"

Ned took an old envelope from his pocket, and wrote:—

"In about ten days or two weeks."

When Dr. John received this communication, he filled a couple of leaves from his notebook with rapid penciling and sent them across the stream. Both boys bent eagerly over this message.

"You must send them in gunny sacks, packed full, and sewed together at the top with stout twine. I'll see that you get the sacks the last of this week. Tie a card to each, with your own name on it, and the name and address of your commission firm. Get them down here every day at half past five in the afternoon. The produce train goes out at seven o'clock every night except Saturday. I'll attend to the shipping."

The note that the doctor had addressed to Hope read as follows:—

MY DEAR HOPE,— The friend of whom I spoke has been to see your father regularly once a week and will continue to do so. There is no change in his condition, and he is as comfortable as he can be made.   Yours obediently,   DR. JOHN.

Two weeks later the boys began picking peas. It was great fun at first, but when several hours had passed, and they found that their backs were getting tired and they had not yet half a sack between them, they were almost ready to give up in despair. They were glad enough when Hope came to their aid, although Martin was sure that she could never stand it for five minutes. When they found that she was picking nearly as many peas as both of them together, they were amazed, and Hope modestly tried to explain away her superior skill by attributing it to the fact that she used her apron for a basket, and thereby kept both hands free for picking. But ah! the little fingers, trained almost from babyhood to a thousand and one household tasks, were defter and quicker than the boys' clumsy hands, hardened now by rough labor.

Hope's skill among the pea-vines resulted in a new division of domestic tasks, for the little maid, seeing the sun high in the heavens, lamented at the thought of leaving her task to prepare luncheon.

"Oh, boys, I do so hate to leave! Couldn't — wouldn't one of you just put the things on the table? There is nothing to be cooked. Everything is ready in the pantry."

"The idea!" sputtered Martin indignantly.

"Martin," said Ned calmly, "this is a question of domestic political economy. It's a question of relative values. If Hope is worth two of us out here, it would be very shallow policy for us to refuse to substitute for her in the house. I pick faster than you, old fellow. You go in the house and get lunch."

Martin laughed good-naturedly and went to the house; and as Martin was a boy who liked to excel in everything he did, he revenged himself upon Hope for her proficiency in picking peas by outshining her in his arrangement of the table.

The boys had the good fortune to get their peas in among the earliest in the market. The first sacks sold at twelve and a half cents a pound, and the price dropped with each succeeding shipment, but they picked seventy-five sacks in all, and when they had finished they found that the venture had netted them nearly three hundred dollars, a sum that seemed a small fortune to them.

When the pea-vines had all been pulled and stacked for fodder, they sent to the nursery for grape cuttings, and planted three acres in vines. They also procured the almond trees they had decided to plant earlier in the year, and for which they had already made preparations, and little by little they got in four acres of young nut trees.

Before the spring was over Dr. John had swung a narrow suspension bridge between the trees. It was a light structure, designed only for foot passengers, neither very firm nor very strong, but it was a vast improvement on the raft, and the children could not express their pleasure and gratitude.

"It is splendid, Dr. John," declared Hope. "But it must have been so much trouble for you, — and — I am afraid it must have cost a lot of money."

"A mere trifle," replied the doctor coolly. "And what is this you boys were saying a little while ago about mending the old trail over the hills?"

"We've got it in pretty good order, sir," replied Ned; "though I don't think we shall have much use for it now."

"But I shall," returned Dr. John, with a slight grimace. "There is a family living a mile or two back of you that is perpetually sending for me in the dead of night. Sometimes the trouble is a toothache, sometimes a little cold or fever, very often a sore finger or toe, — the boys are always getting hurt with their guns. But the crisis invariably comes on late at night, and this old trail is going to save me miles of travel."

"Is it the McCrarys?" asked Ned, laughing.

"Yes, it is the McCrarys," smiled the doctor; "and I should n't wonder if they'd be very neighborly with you when they find they can get down here without much trouble. The McCrarys always have plenty of time to spare, but not much besides. You'll pay a heavy tax yet for opening that trail."

CHAPTER XV.

HOPE AND THE BIRDS.

WHILE Ned and Martin were busy with their outdoor labor, Hope found occupation and entertainment in a variety of delightful ways. During the first days of March the song-birds all re-appeared.

The first of the year had been the signal for many of them to hide away in mysterious nooks, leaving only the titmouse, the meadow lark, and a few other sweet-voiced but shy songsters.

But when the trees came into blossom, the air was again glad with music. First came the dainty goldfinches, with song so faint and sweet that it seemed to melt into the air with the flutter of their green and golden wings. Next came the linnets, the female quiet and domestic in her garb of gray, but with bright eyes that never failed to single out the most desirable location for raising her young brood; the male brilliant and imperious, with his crimson crest and breast and his clear, sustained song. And then all of the feathered tribe seemed to settle down at once on Home Ranch: wrens, yellowhammers, kingbirds, woodpeckers, bluebirds, blue jays, humming-birds, gold-winged blackbirds, sparrows, and a host of others, some of which not even the scientific people have yet named.

Hope knew all the birds' secrets. She watched their love-making and their quarreling, their absurd jealousies, their battles and their merry-makings. She knew of the wren's nest beside the smoke-house door; of the meadow larks' nests on the ground in the pasture; of the titmouse's nest in the rushes by The Brook; of the robins' nest in the walnut tree; of the goldfinches' nests in apple and plum trees; of the linnets' nests anywhere and everywhere within convenient range of the orchard.

A pair of humming-birds, that hovered perpetually about the house, greatly perplexed her for a while. They were the most marvelous little creatures that ever wore feathers, being scarcely larger than fair-sized butterflies, and tricked out in glossy plumage of bronze and green, glowing with a metallic lustre, while collars of the most brilliant ruby color encircled their throats.

One day the boys, coming in from their work in the vineyard, met Hope, her eyes shining, and her lips parted with excitement.

"I've found them out! I've found them out," she cried. "Come with me; but step, — oh, ever so softly! or you'll frighten them."

She led the way to the climbing rose at the front of the house, and carefully lifting a branch, motioned to the boys to look under it. There, hidden in the leafy covert, no higher than the young girl's chin, was the daintiest nest ever seen, made of soft cotton from the pussy willows by The Brook, interwoven with the finest grasses and green mosses, and embroidered with one shining golden thread. And there was wee mother humming-bird, watching them a moment with bright, inquiring eyes, then darting off and poising in the air just above their heads, uncovering two tiny eggs about the size of buckshot, lying in a downy hollow like a thimble.

"I saw her take the thread of yellow silk about a week ago," whispered Hope breathlessly; "I threw it out, with some bits of cotton and some raveled yarn. I do it every day, — it is such fun to see the birds scurry off with them, looking over their shoulders to see if I am watching. They've grown to expect it, and it helps me to find the nests. Two linnets were fighting over the piece of bright silk, and the humming-bird came down like a flash and carried it off."

"If you could only tame her!" suggested Martin. "I've read of setting a little honey or sugar and water in the window, and that birds will learn to come for it."

Hope tried the experiment, and not only the birds came for the sweet food, but it attracted any number of gorgeous butterflies, of every size and of all the colors of the rainbow. These beautiful creatures were not content to sip their sweets on the window sill, but soon learned to dart into the room, and they circled around the little woman who looked after their tastes with such consideration, frequently alighting on her head and shoulders, and even upon her hands. But after a few weeks the wild flowers on the hills allured them, and the flies arrived in such swarms that Hope was constrained to put aside the tempting dainties. She resolved, however, to have a "butterfly month" every spring, and this pretty custom became a part of the established order at Home Ranch.

CHAPTER XVI.

THE OLD ORCHARD.

The children did not know how much they had missed Dr. John until now that he resumed his old habit of coming over once a day to look in upon them and advise them, poor farmer though he claimed to be. The day after the hanging bridge was put in place the doctor found his way to the orchard where the boys were hoeing, and looked about, with hearty approval, at the changes they had made. The trees were no longer ill-shapen and straggling, but had been carefully trimmed, while young trees had been planted in all the vacant spaces. Beside the old trees were two rows of fig-suckers that Martin had set out.

"The old fig-trees don't look to me exactly healthy," remarked Ned. "If you'll just look at them closely, doctor, you'll see there are little bunches coming out in the axil of every leaf. They look as if they might have been made by some insect, but I've looked high and low, and I can't find a sign of a bug or worm."

"Why, my boy," exclaimed Dr. John, "those are the figs."

"The figs! They haven't had a sign of a blossom yet."

"I remember, I remember," cried Martin. "The book says the florescence is inside of the fig."

The doctor quietly cut open a fig and handed it to the boys, with a little magnifying glass. True enough, there were the myriads of tiny blossoms clustered about the hollow centre of the fruit.

A little farther on they came to a row of perhaps a dozen and a half trees, heavily loaded with green fruit, and so surrounded with props that they resembled the sacred banian-trees of India, which send down roots and grow new trunks from the tips of the horizontal branches.

"What in the world is this?" demanded the doctor.

"Those are our apricots. Are n't we going to have a pile, though! You can't see some of the branches at all, the fruit is so clustered around them."

"It really seems as if we can't get enough props for them," sighed Ned. "It keeps Martin and me busy a couple of hours every morning, and it's getting hard to find room for the props. Just see how those branches up above are bending down. They'll break before to-morrow if we don't prop them."

"How would it do to put some of the branches in slings?" suggested Dr. John.

"In slings? I don't quite understand, sir," said Ned.

Ned looked keenly at Dr. John, and saw that he put up his hand and pulled his mustache to cover a smile that bade fair to expand into a laugh.

"Dr. John, what ought we to do?"

"Boys, did you never hear of such a thing as thinning fruit?"

"Oh, we don't want to do anything like that," protested Martin. "The papers say the apricot crop is going to be very light this year. They're going to be our main crop, and we're going to save every one."

"Do people ever 'thin' fruit, doctor?" asked Ned.

"Well, yes, they do," replied the doctor. "In fact, it's quite the custom. During this month and next thinning fruit will be the chief occupation on almost every ranch throughout the county."

"But the idea!" cried Martin, who could not brook the thought of parting with any of his cherished apricots before their time. "Just as if the trees did n't know best what they were able to stand. Is n't nature the best guide, Dr. John?"

"Nature has had possession of this orchard for about seven years, and you can see what a job she has made of it," retaliated the doctor. "Nature, young man, knows nor cares nothing about supplying the demands of our city markets. She is dominated by one purpose: the propagation of species. The more a tree or plant is neglected, the greater its fecundity. All its strength and vitality are directed to that purpose, although it is sometimes its fate to be stamped out of existence by other plants still more prolific and persistent, like the weeds that had possession of the soil when you came here. If you want apricots of a marketable size, you must thin them out."

"Well, I, for one, shall be glad to be relieved of the trouble of hunting up props," declared Ned; "and they will make excellent firewood, Martin. How many apricots would you leave on a branch, doctor?" he asked, taking hold of a bough of the tree under which they stood, and commencing to pluck off the fruit.

"The fruit should be at least four or five inches apart on an apricot tree. Peaches are always thinned to a distance of seven or eight inches. Of course, it is necessary to exercise a little judgment. If you find a stout branch with the fruit all clustered in one spot, it would be reasonable to leave two or three close together. Be careful not to pull off any little leaf-twigs with the fruit. It takes a good deal of courage, boys, to thin fruit as one ought. Mr. Abbott tells a good story of a young Scotchman who came out here last year, and whom he set to work thinning fruit in his orchard. The man worked on for a time in open disapproval. When he had removed about a third of the necessary amount of fruit, he 'struck' work, and surveyed the tree and the ground beneath it. 'I've thrawn awa' a' tha' gude fruit I'm gaun to!' he announced, with dignified decision, and walked off from the ranch, and was seen no more."

CHAPTER XVII.

MAKING IMPROVEMENTS.

By the middle of May the last rains of the season had long since passed. The ground the Austins had under cultivation had received its last harrowing, and presented the smooth, crummy appearance so dear to the eyes of the California farmer.

The boys now had before them six months of comparative leisure, which would be broken in upon only by the harvesting of their light fruit crop, in mid-summer.

For summer was upon them with the middle of May. The temperature, whose average had been steadily raised each month of the year, attained a really genial warmth. On the hills all the sunny exposures were brilliant with wild flowers of every hue, and in the shaded gorges and on the north side of the hills beautiful ferns spread their delicate tracery of green against the deeper emerald of moss, or the warm browns and yellows of lichen-bespattered rocks. Lush grasses, on which the cattle loved to feed, carpeted the openings between the trees on the mountains, and grew rank and high over the little pasture on Home Ranch.

The sycamores, alders, madronas, maples, and

willows along The Brook rejoiced in their summer foliage, and their fresh greens stood out in beautiful relief against the sombre tones of the evergreen oak. Orchard and vineyard were marching on to the fruition of their spring promises; not with the unseemly haste of northern and New England summers, but with stately, measured step, as if they realized the generous allotment of time nature had given them, in which to complete their season's task.

Early in the season Ned and Martin began to excavate a reservoir to hold back the water of the spring, in order to get a sufficient head to irrigate the figs in the old orchard. The doctor came upon them one day when they were engaged in this work.

"My patience, boys, what a hole you have made!" he cried. "Don't you think you have rather overdone it? Twenty or thirty thousand gallons would have given you a big supply. This will hold fifty or sixty thousand, at the least."

Ned looked very much abashed.

"Have you any idea how much cement it's going to take, Dr. John, or how much lime and sand we ought to mix with it? The encyclopædia is very free in telling all about its composition, but very indefinite about proportions."

"I can't say, I'm sure," replied Dr. John, shaking his head and knitting his brows. "I am afraid it will cost a small fortune."

The boys looked at each other in a crestfallen

silence. Suddenly Dr. John's eye brightened and his manner changed.

" Hello ! What is this ? "

He kicked a hard, rock-like substance with his foot, and then stooped and picked up a lump.

" Oh, that ? That sticky old clay ! It did seem as if we would never get it out. The bottom 's all made up of it. Just see that big pile over there. It 's all one solid lump," explained Martin.

Dr. John stepped over to the pile of clay indicated by the boy, and, breaking away the outer crust, possessed himself of a moist and plastic lump. Moulding this into a hollow cup, he dipped it into the spring and held it out, filled with water, in his hand.

" Well ? " said Ned inquiringly.

" Do you see a leak anywhere ? "

" No, sir. It 's water-tight."

" What did you want the cement for ? "

" Why, to keep the water from soaking into the earth; to make the reservoir water-tight. Oh, I see. Martin, what geese we have been ! What better lining do we want than this very clay that has been bothering us so ? "

So the reservoir was completed, and by the middle of the summer the fig-trees were copiously irrigated twice or three times a week, but not in time to save the first crop, which had already fallen to the ground. The boys supplemented the good work by running a second water-channel, lined with the impervious clay, down to the kitchen door, where they made a little reservoir to supply water for household uses.

They harvested a light fruit crop from the old orchard that year, and, although it was by no means of the first quality, it happened that the fruit crop was everywhere light that year, and they were thus enabled to secure good prices. The fig-trees drank up the water sent down to them, like thirsty camels that had crossed a broad and desolate waste; but the great leaves hung like so many gigantic sheltering hands over the smooth gray branches, and there was no further sign of fruit or blossom.

One day, about the last of September, the children passed through the orchard on their way to The Brook, where they had been at work for some days, preparing material for a rude fence to shut off a corral for the cattle and to protect their winter's crops. Martin ran over to look at the irrigating ditch and to see if the water was running freely in it, for they had lifted the gate that morning. Quite by chance he looked over towards the trees.

"Come here, Ned!" he cried exultantly.

Ned came and looked, and there, in the axils of the huge leaves, were tiny green bunches.

"Do you think they'll come to anything?" asked Martin anxiously.

"I don't know. It seems pretty late in the season."

But they did come to something. Day after day

the boys watched the trees, as they went back and forth, dragging logs and timber for the fence. So rapidly did the fruit " come on " that they felt it prudent to order a couple of dozen fig-boxes, and they had them ready none too soon. The figs expanded, softened, took on color, and were ready for picking in two weeks from the time they were first discovered. Better still, as soon as the trees were relieved of the ripe fruit the small green figs began to swell. On the 21st of October, twelve days after the first picking, a second crop was ready for market, and this excelled the first in quantity and quality. On the 2d of November, precisely twelve days later, the third crop, less in quantity but of even finer quality, was gathered. On the eighth of November, seven days later, the last crop, a straggling remnant, was sold at good prices. Altogether, they netted upwards of nineteen dollars from four trees, and were jubilant, as they well might be, over the success of this little crop.

When they came to count up the profits from their entire fruit crop that season, they found that, small as the sum was, it very nearly covered their living expenses for the whole summer, leaving the money they had received for the peas almost untouched.

During the summer months the boys carried out a long-cherished plan, and entered upon a systematic course of home study, aided by Dr. John's advice, and by an eastern educational society, of which they became corresponding members.

Hope had taken her share in the out-door work, as well as the boys, and there had been a division of household tasks as unexpected as it was pleasant for the young girl. The new life had a magical effect on the slight child, and the roses bloomed in her cheeks for the first time since her mother died.

CHAPTER XVIII.

TWO SURPRISES.

THERE came a time in the fall when the boys were at a loss to know what to do with the long hours that hung heavily upon them.

"Let's prospect. There are lots of rocks about here. We might find a gold or silver lode. Anyway, we could start a cabinet of stones and bugs and things," proposed Martin.

"I'd enjoy that kind of thing as much as you, if my mind were only free, Martin," rejoined Ned. "But I have a feeling all the time that we ought to be working to some purpose. Just see the way we're living: sleeping in the only sitting-room we've got. It isn't nice for Hope, and it isn't nice for us. I wish there was some way we could tack on an extra room."

"We could do it if we had the lumber," said Martin confidently.

"But we haven't, and we can't afford it, either; even if we could contrive to get it over here. But if we could even make it out of logs; now that seems feasible. There are any number of young saplings down by the stream, and we could plaster the chinks with clay. You know there's an extra door already, leading out of the front room, that we could use. A window would be easily enough managed."

The boys went down to the brook, taking axe and hatchet, and blazing a mark on young trees of suitable size, as they came across them. There was a little piece of woodland bordering on the stream at the extreme southern corner of their place, that they had never explored. Searching for straight and shapely young trees, they followed the stream down farther than they had ever gone before, and went out on a little neck of land that projected sharply into the water, where the stream made a sudden bend and left the hills, which seemed to crowd it too closely, to escape into the free and open valley.

The lower side of this neck of land abutted on an out-jutting ledge of rock that overhung the water. The upper side was bordered with tall trees that seemed to interlace and form an impenetrable hedge. Ned walked over to see what prospects there were in this direction. He climbed into one of the trees, in order to see what lay beyond.

"Martin, come here!" he cried in excitement.

Martin's nimble limbs soon helped him to his brother's side, whence he looked down upon an astonishing sight. The file of tall forest trees had acted like the booms constructed in the lumber regions of the north to catch logs carried down by the winter freshets. Piled up against them was a goodly share of the débris of the flood, a fantastic medley of skeleton trees, uprooted chaparral, fence rails and posts, heavy timber, planks, — lumber of every description; assorted odds and ends, enough to build a house, had there only been more of a kind.

"Do you mind giving me a pinch, Martin, to see whether I'm awake? It's altogether too Crusoe-like," declared Ned. "You remember how it was with Robinson: whenever he was in great need of anything, it was sure to turn up right to his hand."

"Crusoe-like or no," rejoined Martin, "we've got our room, and firewood enough for a year to come, if we can ever untangle it."

It is no easy matter for two boys, who have never had any experience in building, to put up a dwelling, or a portion of a dwelling, so that it shall be safe for people to live in it. The boys puzzled long over the framing of the timbers, being finally helped out of their quandary by Dr. John, who was a practical observer, and knew just enough to show them how to put the framework together in such a way as to make it firm and solid.

The room grew but slowly, for much of the work was really beyond the boys' strength, and they were obliged to take frequent rests. They built up the walls breast-high with hewn saplings, and above these they clapboarded with broad planks, the lower edge of each overlapping the top of the next below, so as to shed water.

It was a rough specimen of building when they had done, but it was substantial, and answered their purpose nicely. The room was much larger than they had meant to make it, for they wanted to do the most with their lumber, and could not bear to cut off an unnecessary foot. It looked rougher from the inside than from without, and Hope, with the instinct of a neat housewife, pointed out the ledges that would catch dust, and the attractive prospect it offered to spiders and cockroaches.

After a short consultation, the boys went down to the village store and bought a whole piece of figured chintz, at eight cents a yard. This they cut into appropriate lengths, which Hope stitched together on the machine, and when it was ready they tacked it into place, completely covering the ceiling and the walls. It was a pretty piece of cloth, gray, with a little pink figure, and the effect was really very pleasant when the room was draped with it. They had made one window, for which they bought frame and sashes, and when Hope took an old white sheet, and, gathering the top on a cord, tacked it into place, catching it back with a piece of faded pink ribbon from among her own stores, and dressed the bed with a white spread and clean linen, they voted it the very prettiest room in the house.

They next gave their attention to the outside of the house, and plastered the crumbling adobe with handfuls of moist clay, but this gave it such a mottled look that they were quite ashamed of it when they were done.

A few days later Ned returned home, after half

a day's absence, to find Martin standing on a rude ladder they had used when building, a large bucket hooked upon one of the rounds, busily at work upon the side of the house, plying a whitewash brush that had done service about the chicken house.

"Hold on, Martin!" Ned shouted, as soon as he got within speaking distance. "Don't daub it up with whitewash, of all things. That will be ghostly."

"Go around and look at the front of the house, where it is dry," said Martin coolly, without ceasing his work.

It was such a piece of presumption for Martin to order him about that Ned mechanically obeyed, overcome by the boy's effrontery. He found the entire front of the house an even, cool gray.

"How did you manage it, youngster?" demanded Ned, when he returned, greatly puzzled, for they had voted that the cost of paint was entirely out of the question.

No answer.

"Find a mine of natural paint in the hills?"

Still no answer.

"Rob a paint store?"

The young artist turned, gave the impertinent questioner one withering look, and resumed his task.

"Oh, come now. Don't be too hard on a fellow. Is it oil paint, or is it water color, or what in the name of creation is it?"

"Lampblack."

"Lampblack! Lampblack is black as soot, and this is a neat gray. Are you crazy, Martin?"

"Ask Hope. I'm too busy."

"Yes," said Hope, appearing on the scene, gently triumphant. "It is lampblack, Ned. Just whitewash, made with the lime you had left from the chicken-house, with the least bit of lampblack stirred in. Martin and I studied it up together."

Rain fell about the middle of November, and one morning during the first storm, Ned came puffing into the kitchen, in the midst of a driving shower, with a fawn-colored something in his arms, whose great eyes looked up to Hope with the eloquent appeal of a young deer.

"Can't you give it a place in the kitchen to-day, Hope? It is so wet and cold, and can't stand on its legs; but they say you ought always to take them away from the mother at once."

"Ned Austin!" cried Hope, dropping toast and toasting-fork into the fire, in her excitement, and falling on her knees beside the little creature, as Ned laid it tenderly upon the floor. "You don't mean — Oh, is n't it lovely! You pretty, helpless little darling? It is n't — Oh, Ned! It can't be"—

"Beauty's calf? But it is," rejoined Ned. "And you 'll let it stay in the house to-day?"

"*To-day!*" Hope's voice was scathing. "*It shall stay in the house all winter.*"

"The idea!" shouted Ned, and Martin joined him in his hearty laughter.

"You absurd little girl!" he contrived to say after a while. "The idea of raising a calf in the house is ridiculous. You can keep it as long as you like. But here's the milk-pail; put it on the stove, Martin, and warm it a little. We've got to teach the little thing to eat."

With the air of veteran dairymen the two boys went to work, Ned holding the calf's muzzle down in the milk, while Martin inserted one of his fingers in her mouth. It was wonderful how quickly the little creature understood, and began to take the milk. The coffee was cold, and the toasting-fork had done its last service when rescued from the bed of coals, but the three children were in ecstasies of delight, and even old dog Tray, who had risen from his post beside the breakfast-table and come forth to sniff at the intruder, wagged his tail in interested approval.

There is no animal, unless it be a wee human baby, quite as frail and weak as a little Jersey calf when first it opens its eyes upon this world. Calves of common stock often go galloping over a field a few hours after birth, but this little animal lay helpless and exhausted, the spark of life seeming to glow and fade by turns, while its beautiful eyes appeared to beseech help and sympathy.

The boys brought in hay and made it a bed in the corner of the kitchen, and Hope scarcely dared trust it out of her sight, but when she was performing her daily tasks in the other rooms, kept running to the kitchen to see if the frail creature was still alive. For two successive mornings, although they did not confess it to each other, each of the three tiptoed to the kitchen at break of day, with solemn expectancy in their faces, fully expecting to find their delicate charge stiff and dead.

On the morning of the fourth day, they were aroused by a prolonged growl from old Tray, which resounded throughout the house. Hope sprang out of bed, wrapped a shawl about her, and flew out of her room, only to encounter the boys, barefooted and vainly trying to fasten their suspenders as they raced towards the kitchen and flung the door open.

They were greeted by a startling and dramatic sight. The bed of hay in the corner was empty, but before the stove lay old dog Tray, in his accustomed place, and over him hovered a spectral apparition, very shaky on its legs, but with Beauty's own bland mischief in its eyes, looking down upon the poor dog, who seemed paralyzed with astonishment and terror.

It was plain that Tray thought some strange phantom from canine dreamland had come to haunt him in his waking hours, for he did not stir leg or foot, but, at the opening of the door, turned such a look of distress upon his young protectors that they screamed with merriment.

The calf, distracted from her victim by this sound, threw up her head, gave them one look, and then charged at them, scattering the little group right and left. She raced through the front room to the boys' room, kicking up her heels as she vanished from sight; then reappeared, caromed into Hope's room, bounced back, gave a series of exultant leaps around the room where they stood, darted out into the kitchen again, made a rush at Tray, who slunk under the table to escape her, knocked a pile of milk-pans off the stove hearth, and was finally seized by the boys and brought to a halt, her great eyes shining with the same calm light.

"Oh, horrors!" cried Hope. "Boys, do you think she has gone mad?"

"Not a bit of it!" laughed Ned. "She's perfectly level-headed, Hope. Saner than we were. We ought to have known better than to try to keep her in the house."

"*Don't* you want to keep her in the house all winter?" jested Martin.

"Oh, no, no, no! Take her out just as quick as you can. It's a mercy there's a whole dish in the house," answered the young girl, who could not shake off the horror of what might have been. "Oh, you slyboots! I never would have believed it of you — never."

"Slyboots shall be her name. You've christened her, Hope," said Ned, who had finally got a rope around the neck of the little heifer calf, and was hauling her, by slow degrees, towards the door.

CHAPTER XIX.

A TRIP TO THE CITY.

The second Christmas after they settled on Home Ranch, Hope and Martin went down to see their father. Discouraged by Ned's reception, and fearful that their presence might somehow work harm to the invalid, they had sent messages and the simple gifts at their command, and received in return the reports of Dr. John's friend, which came regularly every week. But now the doctor himself advised that they should go.

The sick man had been watching for them all the morning. Every time that the door of the long ward opened, his eyes had turned toward it with an expectant look. He was lying in a great invalid chair, whose carved frame and soft upholstery contrasted sharply with the simplicity about it. At length his quickened hearing caught the sound of young voices in the hall. The door opened, and there stood his little Hope, looking down the ward in timid inquiry.

How fair and tall and womanly she had grown! His heart yearned over her, and he longed to clasp her in his arms, and shower blessings on her dear young head. He could only lie and look at her, his eyes eloquent with the love and emotion his lips could not express.

A sick man in the next cot started up wildly as the innocent girl ran by, with her arms outstretched, a bunch of flowers in her hand.

"The Angel of Light!" he cried, and fell back on the pillow, where he watched her with wild, rapt gaze, muttering the words over and over again.

Others in the ward propped themselves up on one elbow to rejoice in the glad vision. The father alone could give no sign of the joy that filled his heart.

Ah, well! It was soon over, and he had only fair memories to remind him of his children's presence. The delirious patient in the next cot was still raving about the "angel of light," and died with the cry upon his lips. The bunch of flowers was still there, in the glass where she had placed them; soon they would fade and die.

He alone outlived his usefulness. Day and night he waited with long-deferred hope for the coming of the King.

The children stopped to speak with the physician in charge of the ward, as they went out.

"It was so good of you to get that nice chair for father, sir," said Hope. "He seems so comfortable in it, and it must be such a change for him, after lying all night in bed in one position."

The physician looked embarrassed. It would not do to let the matter pass in that way. Other patients were within hearing. It might breed discontent in the ward.

"The hospital board has no money to waste on such luxuries," he said shortly. "That was sent here by your father's friend."

"Father's friend?"

"Yes, the gentleman who comes to see him every Sunday."

"Oh, Dr. John's friend," said Martin; and when the children reached home that night and saw Dr. John, they broached the subject to him.

"Dr. John, your friend has brought father a beautiful chair. It is very kind of him, but don't you think we ought to pay for it? We would like to."

"Not at all, not at all," said the doctor gruffly. "Let him do it if he wants to. He can afford it better than you."

"He must be a very generous man, I am sure, to do so much for a stranger," said Hope.

"On the contrary, he is one of the most selfish men I know," declared Dr. John. "He has done it for nothing in the world but his own pleasure. Oh, I know the man. Let me manage him."

"I must say I think Dr. John does n't half appreciate that friend of his," said Martin, when they had turned away. "I 'll tell you what, I go more on him than I do on Dr. John. You don't know everything about Dr. John."

"Why, Martin," cried Hope, in amazement. "And just think! If it had n't been for Dr. John he would never have known anything about father."

"Yes, that's so. But it's very easy to do good things by proxy," insisted Martin.

"By proxy! Martin Austin! I should think you'd be ashamed of yourself. Perhaps Dr. John has helped us by proxy. Oh, yes, he's helped us by proxy all along, — made us welcome here, and looked after us in all sorts of ways, and built the foot bridge, and helped us with encouragement and advice, by proxy, right along!"

By the time Hope had finished this incoherent and indignant speech, she was wiping the tears from her eyes, and Martin was ready to prostrate himself in the dust before her, to appease her and his own conscience.

Yet only the week before, Martin had taken another ride to Oakland with the doctor, and he felt that he had been installed as Dr. John's confederate. He was beginning to understand what it was to " be a man with a history."

It meant a dark, disgraceful secret to be concealed. It meant fear and distrust of one's fellowman. It meant underhand, humiliating ways of doing business. It meant suspicion of others and contempt of one's self. Martin wished with all his heart that the doctor had no history.

The first year of experiment and struggle was safely past, and the boys felt that they might now look forward to an era of prosperity and comfort.

Yet serious trouble was close at hand, and Hope, wise, prudent little Hope, was to bring disaster upon them.

CHAPTER XX.

HOPE'S EMBEZZLEMENT.

AFTER the money for the peas had been laid aside in the spring, it was really wonderful how nearly their income had kept pace with their expenses. When December had come and gone, and the new crop was planted, they had drawn less than twenty dollars from the two hundred and odd they had received from their spring sales.

Ned carefully estimated their expenses for the coming spring, including new suits for himself and Martin, and a liberal contingency fund, and found that he still had a surplus of a hundred dollars. He gave this into Hope's hands, saying : —

"There, little sister, I think you should have command of something. There must be some things you need."

Hope's eyes glistened as her hand closed on the great double eagles.

"And may I spend just a little of it for myself?"

Her voice was so eager that Ned was smitten with self-reproach.

"Why, Hope! spend every penny of it if you

like. What misers we boys have been! You've been wanting something in the way of clothes and would n't tell us.".

"No, no, — not clothes!" corrected the young girl earnestly. "Flowers."

"Flowers?" repeated both boys in chorus.

"Yes, flowers, — roses. Oh, I've wanted them so much, and there's such a beautiful place for them along the path to The Brook. If I only could go to Mr. Abbott's and buy some outright" —

"Why, of course, Hope," interrupted Ned. "It's high time you had some pleasure for yourself. Go to-morrow."

It was a glad day for Hope when she set out to buy her roses, armed with a capacious basket.

The gentle nurseryman met her with a pleasant smile.

"And what wants my little maid with the big basket?"

"Some roses, please, Mr. Abbott," replied Hope in a sprightly tone, for it really raised the young girl's spirits to find herself out in the world, negotiating for these coveted treasures.

"Roses?" returned the old man. "And what kind of roses do you want?"

"Why, if you please," said Hope, "I think — I would like all kinds."

Mr. Abbott laughed, a pleased, indulgent laugh, that could not have wounded the feelings of anybody.

"My dear," he said, "I am afraid you can't find them here. How many kinds of roses does this little woman suppose there are in cultivation?"

"Why, I thought — I supposed," said Hope, "about a dozen, — possibly two dozen."

"Say two thousand, my child, and you will be nearer right," explained Mr. Abbott gravely.

"Two thousand!" repeated the young girl, dismayed.

"Double that, — and the number is increasing every year," he continued. "But now let us see what we can find. I think I have perhaps thirty or forty varieties that I have picked up from time to time."

Mr. Abbott was even better than his word. He went the rounds of the place with Hope, and in a short time forty-two plants, representing as many standard varieties of roses, were snugly packed in the willow basket. So Hope handed him four dollars from her little purse, with as great a pride and a loftier pleasure than if she had been an empress, negotiating for some rare and costly fabric.

"I really think," remarked the nurseryman, as he led his visitor to his trim little office, to make out a receipt in due form, "that some one might make money by going into roses on a considerable scale. I don't know of any nursery on the coast that makes a specialty of them. Besides propagating plants for sale, there could be a very decent income secured by selling cut flowers to the city florists."

Hope's eyes brightened with a new light, and the flush in her cheeks deepened.

"Mr. Abbott," she asked, as he handed her the receipt, "who — does — keep — all kinds — of roses?"

"I don't know of any one house in the country," replied the old gentleman, "but there are several eastern rose-growers of high repute who have a very large selection. How would you like to carry home some of their catalogues? They send them to me every year. You will find them very attractive books; in fact they are so very pretty and attractive that, as I don't care to go any deeper into roses myself, I had quite as lief get rid of their temptations. Perhaps you would like to send on for one of their dollar collections, my dear. They are really worth having."

He put together several nicely illustrated pamphlets as he spoke, and tucked them in the willow basket, quite unconscious of the firebrand he was touching to the young girl's imagination.

There was a lot of ground intersected by The Brook path that had been carefully ploughed, and that was admirably suited for ornamental purposes, and Hope at once appropriated it for a rose garden. It so happened that she wished to mass the colors by themselves, but that she could not remember the description of all of them, and she was obliged to consult the catalogues to find out. Now it chanced that the one she took up was the most bewitching of all, a thick, magazine-like book, upon the cover of which a beautiful pink rose was pictured. Turning the leaves, she came upon some rich-colored plates, representing the latest novelties in roses, and at sight of these the child gave little exclamations of delight. She became so absorbed in the book that it was not until she heard the sound of the boys' voices at the house, and looked up to see smoke curling from the kitchen chimney, that she realized how late it was and bethought herself of her neglected duties. Hurriedly "heeling in" the plants, a process which consisted simply in laying them together and covering the roots with a layer of damp earth, she ran up to the house.

This was only the beginning. A few days later Hope sent off orders for three one-dollar collections of ever-blooming roses, addressed to as many different florists. Two weeks later the plants arrived by mail, carefully packed in damp moss and protected from the journey across the continent by many wrappings of paper and cotton wadding, as well as wooden casings. When she opened them they looked as fresh as if they had just been taken from the pots.

And now it became noticeable that wherever Hope went a pile of prettily illustrated pamphlets was sure to be close by. In the kitchen, washing dishes, kneading bread, peeling apples, overseeing her cooking, darning, sewing on buttons, whatever her task, an open book was always before her, and tucked in her apron pocket were paper and pencil, whereon she made copious notes. The boys jested her on her fits of abstraction and the random answers she made them, but she smiled wisely back and gave no hint of the secret purpose that possessed her mind.

For, little by little, yielding to the insidious influences of the charming catalogues, Hope became fixed with a wild ambition.

She wanted to get all the different kinds of roses.

CHAPTER XXI.

HOPE'S INDICTMENT.

THE boys, deep in their own plans and duties, paid little attention to Hope's flowers. They knew that she spent all her spare time in her own little garden, and they noticed the frequent arrival of packages by mail, bearing the stamp of eastern florists; but as fifty roses were packed in the same compass as one, and weighed little more, and as they never gave more than a careless look towards her growing plantation, they had but a slight idea of the extent of their sister's investment.

It all came out one evening in March. They were sitting together in their cosy room, Martin deep in a volume of the Encyclopædia, Ned frowning over his account book, and Hope, as usual, busy with her catalogues. She had come very nearly to the end of both her money and her roses. Out of the nine hundred varieties named in the lists, she had now six hundred and more, and as the plants had been planted at the most favorable season of the year, all of them, with the exception of three or four delicate varieties, were thriving finely.

Her one anxiety now was to make the money

she had left cover the cost of the remaining roses, a very knotty problem for a young girl unused to financiering, for the beautiful moss roses, and some of the rarest teas and hybrids, the most costly of all, were among them.

"Well, Martin," said Ned, "we've gone away beyond our calculations this time. The repairs on the plough and the new seed planter made a big hole in our surplus."

"We had to have them," commented Martin, looking up from his book.

"Yes, and we've got to have other things. You and I have got to have new boots, or go barefooted this spring. Our bran ran out to-day, and the cow must be properly fed if we wish her milk to keep up. It does seem as if those pea-pods never will fill out this spring. Martin, we're bankrupt! The only thing for us to do is to fall back on Hope's bounty."

Although Ned had placed the hundred dollars in Hope's hands and wanted her to feel that she could draw freely upon it, both of the boys had understood, and supposed she did, that it was in some measure a trust fund, and they had confidence that the little woman would handle it wisely.

Hope had dropped her pencil and paper when Ned commenced to speak, and stared at him with wide, anxious eyes. She stood up when he finished, and both of the boys wondered at her pale, startled face.

"But, Ned, you said I could have it all — every cent!"

"And I meant it, too, Hope," said Ned apologetically, though secretly wondering to see his generous-hearted sister suddenly become so penurious. "But you see how it is, Hope. Things cost more than I reckoned they would, and a lot of extras came tumbling in. I have n't but eighty-five cents to my name, Hope, and we can't count on anything from our peas before the middle of April. That 's a good four weeks off. I guess thirty dollars will carry us through."

"But I have n't got it," protested Hope, horror-stricken. "I have n't but eleven dollars left. I — I 've spent all the rest."

"Whe-e-ew!"

Ned silenced his impetuous brother with but a single look, but he knit his own brows. "Only eleven dollars left? That 's rough on us, Hope. I did n't know girls' clothes cost so much! But of course it 's all right."

He had entirely forgotten what Hope had said at the time he had given the money into her keeping.

"Clothes! Do you think I 'd go and spend all that money for clothes? Why, Ned, I did n't so much as buy a handkerchief for myself nor a pair of stockings; and mine are darned and darned until there are more darns than stocking to them."

"But what did you spend it for, Hope?" asked Ned in perplexity.

"Flowers, — roses. I told you I would like to. Don't you remember? Though I never thought then — I didn't know there were so many, or that they would cost so much to buy."

"A hundred dollars for that scrubby little lot of plants down by The Brook path! Well, I must say it takes a girl to throw away a man's hard earnings!" Martin burst out angrily, and the next minute most unexpectedly found himself out on the front porch.

But when Ned turned to look for Hope, she had disappeared.

"Poor little girl!" he said to himself. "She has toiled so hard, for more than a year and a half, without any of the amusements other girls of her age enjoy. Martin and I have worked together, while she's been shut up in the house alone, half the time. Small wonder she turned to flowers for companionship. We've been trying to make a woman of her before her time."

He went out of doors in search of her, and some instinct led him to where she stood, with her arms clasping the mottled trunk of the old leaning sycamore, down by the roses, crying as if her heart would break. Something rose in his own throat at the sight. He recalled, more clearly than before, the heritage of sorrow and care that had descended upon her in childhood; the sickness and death of the dear young mother; the patient manner in which the delicate child had tried to share the duties that had grown too heavy for the mother's failing strength, and then had assumed them wholly, as a sacred trust left by the dead. He remembered the shock of their father's sudden prostration, and the manner in which she had interpreted his wish that they should remain together, and then found a way to carry out the promise they had given him, and bravely upheld her share — yes, more than her share! — of their burdens. And then to think that he and Martin should so wound that gentle heart! It seemed to Ned that in all the world there was nothing quite so pathetic as the figure of the lonely girl, sobbing out her grief and pain in the shadow of the sycamore.

"There, there, little sister!" he said, drawing her arms away from the tree and making her sit down with him on a great, gnarled root which spread over the ground at its base. "I'm so sorry I said a word about the money, Hope. Of course you had a right to spend it as you pleased. Don't worry. We'll get along all right."

"But it was mean in me to do it. It was selfish. It was worse. I knew you didn't expect me to use only just a little. It was — like — being — a thief!"

As Hope hurled this terrible accusation at herself she broke into a fresh storm of sobs.

"Listen, dear," said Ned. "How can one steal their own money, Hope? You had a perfect right to it, and to more, too. Why, Hope, we've handled several hundred dollars since we first came up here, and Mart and I have kept on gobbling up every cent for improvements, and tools, and seed, and fruit trees, and never so much as asked your approval, when I'm sure you had a clear title to a third of it all. We could never have saved a cent of it if it had n't been for you. Just fancy Martin and I up to our elbows in bread dough, or hurrying to wash the dishes so as to get out to plough, or darning a pair of stockings before we pruned a tree, or running in and out of the house to look after our baking while we were planting, or ironing tablecloths and napkins and groaning about the hoeing that needed to be done in the orchard."

Hope laughed a little at this picture, as Ned meant she should, and he took advantage of the moment to tack deftly about to the sore subject they had both avoided.

"Now, little sister, where are your roses? I don't know of any flower I like so well. I am going to get lots of comfort out of them myself. You must show them to me by daylight."

"If you would really like to see them, the moonlight is so bright I think you could now," answered Hope, quite encouraged to think that Ned was not disposed to regard her treasures with the contempt Martin had shown. She led the way down the long rows, carefully laid out with stakes and lines, as she had seen the boys plant their garden vegetables.

"Here are my dark reds," she explained. "The very darkest of them is the Prince Camille de Rohan, and they say that it looks almost black at a little distance. It is a hybrid perpetual, and a shy bloomer. This row is the bright reds. I think the General Jacqueminot and the American Beauty are probably the finest among them, but the Queen's Scarlet must be beautiful, and the Queen of Bedders is a great bloomer. There are so many that they say are very handsome that it is hard to choose, and I shall have to wait for them to bloom before deciding. Here are the pinks. I think there are more of them than of any others, and the very freest bloomers are among them. The La France, — don't you remember that beautiful pink rose the doctor has, that always blooms in mid-winter? That's the La France, and it is called by many the most beautiful of all roses. I have a nice plant right here at the end, — see! And here are the Hermosa, and the Bon Silene, and the Adam, and the Charles Rovolli, and the Appoline, — all rosy pinks and very choice, — and dozens of others! And here are the blush roses. There are not many of them, and I got all there are named in the catalogues. And the whites! Such beauties as some of them must be, Ned. They say the Niphetos has the most beautiful buds of all, long and pointed. But the Bride, and the Puritan, and the white Bon Silene, and the La Marque are very fine and free bloomers. Then there are lots of yellows, all the shades from pale lemon to deep orange color. I put the mixed salmon and pinks together. Oh, I'm just wild to see what the Sunset rose will be like! But the Princess Beatrice, the very choicest and most beautiful of the class, I couldn't get, because it cost so much. And oh, Ned, I've got two ever-blooming moss roses, — the rarest of all. There's only one firm in the United States that has them both."

"Why, you little rose fancier!" laughed Ned. "You've told me more about roses than I ever knew before in my life."

"Do you think they look very 'scrubby,' Ned?" Hope asked anxiously.

"On the contrary," replied Ned, who had been bending down and closely examining the plants from time to time, "I think they are remarkably handsome and vigorous. Hope, what was your idea in getting them?"

Hope could have hugged her big brother, and cried, all in a breath. It was so good of him to think that she might have had a plan.

"Mr. Abbott said he thought somebody might do well if they made a specialty of roses. He thought there might be considerable profit in raising cut flowers for the San Francisco market."

"Mr. Abbott's ideas are worth considering," said Ned. "Have any of them bloomed yet, Hope?"

"Oh, no," said the little girl, as shocked as a mother might be if asked whether a three-months-old baby had begun to walk. "I couldn't think of letting them. Most of them have budded, but I pinched them off. I sha'n't let them bloom a bit before next spring."

"That's an excellent idea. Just the way I treat

my young orchard trees. Let them get plenty of root and a stout growth before they go to work."

Ned was undoubtedly a very soft-hearted fellow, but he registered a vow that night on his way to the house, that he would send away and get the Princess Beatrice, the rose Hope wanted so much to add to her collection, out of the first money that came in from the peas that spring.

CHAPTER XXII.

HARD TIMES.

MARTIN took occasion to apologize to Hope, in a clumsy, boyish fashion, for his angry speech, so that renewed confidence and amity were established among the occupants of Home Ranch. Cheerful as they all tried to be, however, they could not disguise from each other that they had a harsh ordeal before them, which it would require all their pluck to meet.

"If only this warm, showery weather would keep on," exclaimed Ned, one morning late in March, looking out on his field of green peas, which showed a perverse inclination to expend all their vitality in blossoms, without attempting to produce any pods, "I believe our peas would begin to come on inside of ten days. We're going to have a magnificent crop."

But it somehow happens that when one desires most of Nature she gives least. The rains suddenly ceased and were succeeded by a period of unreasonably warm weather, when the hot sunshine baked the earth about the tender vines before the boys could get over the field with cultivator and hoes. Following closely upon this there came a hot "norther," a climatic freak peculiar to California, when hot, dry winds sweep down from the North for three days in succession, parching tender vegetation like a flame. The vines withstood the fiery blast, but the young pods looked flabby and wilted, and recovered only for a slow and stunted growth.

Meanwhile, from sections of the State which had been more favored, sacks upon sacks of green peas began to reach the city in such quantities that the market was soon well stocked.

From eight and ten cents a pound, prices fell to seven, six, five, and three cents, and finally settled down to seventy-five cents a sack, a rate at which no white man could afford to pick and ship them and pay commission on the sales.

"Never mind!" said Ned bravely. "We'll let them ripen, and thrash them all out for seed."

It was well along in May when the peas were sufficiently matured for this purpose, but the boys set to work and beat them with a will, and after a week's hard labor had twenty sacks of seed peas, representing over a ton's weight.

"That'll be eighty dollars, at least," announced Martin.

"Never mind reckoning it up, Martin," replied Ned. "We'll get everything out of them that there is to be had. I'm most anxious to see the flour-bin filled, and some provisions in the pantry. By the way, Hope, I never saw anything hold out like that last sack of flour. It's certainly holding out half as long again as any we ever had before."

"Oh, that all depends — on knowing — just how to economize, Ned," answered Hope, turning away her face, over which a tell-tale blush was creeping.

"We shall have returns from the peas on Tuesday, — only three days more," returned Ned cheerfully. "I can get the check cashed here. Wilkins takes them just the same as money, you know. He'll open his eyes at the sugar and flour and meal and rice and coffee and spices I'm going to lay in on my first order. Why, Hope, I'm getting sick of the sight of bread, sweet and wholesome as it is. I'm fairly ravenous for some of the goodies you used to make when you had things to make them out of."

Hope made no reply.

Neither of the boys suspected that the delicate girl was deliberately reducing her own allowance of food, in atonement for what she looked upon as her unpardonable extravagance in the matter of the roses, and in order to make their provisions hold out until the money from the peas came in. Since their funds had given out and they were unable to buy meat, Hope had insisted upon the boys eating fresh eggs twice a day, to make up for the want of more hearty food, and as their stock of poultry was small, the hens had all they could do to meet the demands upon them.

There were potatoes, — plenty of them; but the young girl, who seemed to have been endowed at her birth with a frail body and a fastidious appetite, had an unaccountable distaste for this most useful, healthful, and desirable of all vegetables. If there had been a skilled cook at hand to dress the simple food up in any of the attractive guises that skilled cooks understand, it is very likely that this prejudice might have been overcome, and that, from relishing potatoes in their more palatable forms, little Hope might have learned to like them in simple ways; but as it was, not even famine could drive the young girl to potatoes in their plain forms, boiled, baked or mashed. Bread and butter she did like, but butter was scarce, and flour cost money and must be made to last. But oh! for just once to sit down to all the bread and butter she could eat!

On the Tuesday that the draft was expected, Ned walked into the village store with an air of confidence and cheer he had not worn for months past. He asked for his mail, and while Mr. Wilkins was looking over the pile of letters tucked in the pigeonhole where he kept the A's, the boy spoke up: —

"By the way, Mr. Wilkins, I see your team is at the door. Can you send a load of goods up to The Brook right away?"

Mr. Wilkins did not appear to notice this inquiry. He had drawn out a postal card, with a written address on one side and a printed blank on the other, the conventional form used by commission men in making reports to the farmers. It was generally believed, throughout the valley, that

Mr. Wilkins was in the habit of reading these postal cards, and more than one of the fruit-growers, proud of their reputation as horticulturists and conscious that they had made shipments a little below the average, which might bring humiliating returns, had been known to hasten down to the post-office at breathless speed, about the time of the arrival of the train, to get their mail when the bag was first opened, and before Mr. Wilkins should have time to read the postals.

Instead of the usual returns, Ned saw the date and signature stamped on the card, and, written across the lines, in a large, clear hand, were the words, not in the choicest of language: —

"*Peas no good.* All full of weevils."

Now whether Mr. Wilkins read the postals or not, if he had done so in this case his conduct certainly justified the act. He leaned over the counter and laid one hand on the arm of Ned, who, looking dazed and troubled, was turning to leave the store.

"Don't you want the things you spoke of, Austin? Your credit's good here. Don't forget that."

"Thank you, Mr. Wilkins," said Ned, in a low voice. "But I'd rather not. Not to-day, anyhow."

Dr. John had come in by another entrance, and was standing a little way off, with a wire cheesebox between him and his young neighbor. He had heard the boy's light-hearted inquiry and remark, then noted his sudden look of discouragement as he read the postal, and — becoming a willful eavesdropper, it must be owned — listened to the subsequent dialogue.

The doctor instantly decided that there was trouble at Home Ranch. After Ned had taken his leave, Dr. John interrogated Mr. Wilkins, and found that gentleman only too ready to talk.

"It's my opinion them young friends of yours are living on air!" frankly declared the grocer. "What else they got to live on? Only one sack of flour since the first of January; no sugar, no oatmeal, no coffee; and the butcher says he haint sold them a pound of meat since March."

Dr. John jumped into his buggy and drove furiously towards home. Where had his own eyes been? What had he been thinking of, that he should have been so blind to the happenings at Home Ranch? He believed it was because there had been so many babies that spring, and the last year's babies were all teething. He would lose no time now in learning the true state of affairs.

He drove directly to the stable and put up his horse, and was walking rapidly off in the direction of The Brook, when Wing's sharp eye espied him.

"Missee Docta'!"

"Well, Wing?"

"Somebody wantee see you. Littee lady in housee."

Dr. John felt almost aggrieved at the news. He had made his daily round of calls all over the country, and wanted a little time to himself. If people would only observe some method about getting sick! Who could the "littee lady" be? Manifestly some one who had come on foot, for there was no horse at the gate or at the carriage steps before the front door.

It was Hope. The busy little housewife so rarely found time to leave home, and was so very timid about crossing the hanging bridge, that Dr. John was surprised to see her. How tall and slight she seemed to have grown in the last few weeks! And how pale she was, with just a little nervous flush in each cheek. That color was not natural; he must look into it afterwards; but first to learn her errand, which she was evidently restless to discharge.

"I am glad to see you, Miss Hope," he said gravely. "What can I do for you to-day?"

"Dr. John, do you think you could lend me twenty dollars, and take this and keep it until I can pay you back?"

She held out a little package wrapped in tissue paper, and, removing the wrappings, brought to view a small open-faced silver watch, which had belonged to her mother.

"Is it worth enough? I am afraid it is very old-fashioned," she said.

The doctor took it and examined it critically, opening the case and looking closely at the works.

"It is a very nice little watch," he said. "I would not hesitate to lend any one twice twenty dollars upon it."

Does the Recording Angel take account of such generous equivocations? If he does, Dr. John will some day have a heavy score to meet.

"Then could you please lend me twenty-five dollars?" asked Hope eagerly. "Because, if you can, I'd like it right now, doctor, so I can get down to the store before "—

As suddenly as the color came it faded, and she slipped down, white and senseless, at the doctor's feet.

"My God, she is starving!" cried the doctor, gathering her in his arms — ah, how light the burden! — and laying her on the sofa.

He touched an electric button and Ah Wing appeared, just as Dr. John had removed the little straw hat and pushed back the waving brown hair from the white forehead, laying a wet cloth across it and sprinkling a little water on her face.

"Gottee clottee blood on blain. You bleed him, he all light," volunteered Ah Wing, who looked upon these proceedings with undisguised disfavor.

Ah Wing liked the doctor very well as a man, but he openly disapproved of him as a physician.

"Wing," said Dr. John, "get me a cup of strong coffee and a slice of buttered toast, as quick as you can."

"You bleed him! Coffee toast no make him well," insisted Ah Wing obstinately.

"Get out of here and do what I tell you, you rascal!" growled the doctor, and Wing, who knew very well the point at which he must draw a line in offering professional advice to his master, beat a hasty retreat.

Hope opened her eyes and looked about her a moment in bewilderment. Then she tried to sit up.

"I don't know what came over me, doctor. I never — felt that way before. I must be going. It's late, and the store — will be closed; and there's the baking to do — and dinner" —

"Hush!" commanded the doctor, so gently and yet with such decision that Hope dared not disobey.

It was so pleasant just to lie still in the comfortable, sunny room; and when Wing came with the cup of fragrant coffee and the great slice of golden-brown toast, and a little jelly that he had added of his own accord, she sat up and ate quite obediently, and wondered to feel so refreshed. That horrible, gnawing sensation she had suffered all day long was entirely gone.

But when she had finished eating, and Wing had carried off the tray, Dr. John came up to her, and there was lightning in his eye.

"Hope," he said shortly, "why did n't you tell me you had n't enough to eat?"

"Oh, doctor!" she cried, "don't tell the boys!" She burst into tears like a detected criminal.

"They had enough. Indeed they had enough," she explained, after she had rallied. "It was only me. I did n't work hard like them. I could stand it better. And, besides, Dr. John, you don't know.

You don't understand how it came about. It was my fault. I used up the money."

And forthwith Hope told the whole story of her embezzlement.

The most she hoped was that Dr. John would say she had done all she could to atone for her fault. Instead, he smiled pleasantly upon her.

"I am like Ned," he said. "I am interested in the roses."

Hope went back home, and the doctor went to the grocer's; but he took with him an order, made out and signed by the young girl, and Ned paid for the goods upon their arrival at the banks of The Brook, so that the young people's dignity was not compromised; but before Hope left Dr. John's house, he made her promise that she would never again allow matters on Home Ranch to come to such a pass without telling him.

"It would grieve me very sorely to think that you had not sufficient confidence in me for that," he said, looking sadly at her.

CHAPTER XXIII.

THE SECOND SEASON.

The second summer, by tacit consent, Hope took her place as a co-worker with her brothers, in all that a quick, active girl was capable of doing, and from this date on the indoor and outdoor work of Home Ranch progressed in a manner quite satisfactory to them all.

They had many bothers that they would not have had if they had been grown people, and yet as a rule they managed to set them aside as only children can. Grown people — the best of them — are slaves to many customs and conventionalities that young people are not afraid to defy. So it came about that on days when the boys were glad to have Hope's help out of doors, they did not hesitate to help a little with the housework, and they took pains to dispense with everything that made unnecessary work.

In her housework Hope actually made a study of doing things in the shortest possible ways, which everybody knows no really proper housewife would ever tolerate. She had an old-fashioned cook-book, written and published years before, but still much after the style of modern cook-books, whose ruling purpose seems to be to show what elaborate dishes can be elaborately wrought from simple materials. Hope was obliged to consult this book, because she did not know how to cook many things, and it was all the authority she had; but she had an iniquitous way of circumventing its recipes.

"*Six eggs, yolks and whites beaten separately, for half an hour, with a wire whisk.* What an absurd idea! When you can beat them, and beat them, and beat them, and they will never get a particle lighter after the first five minutes. *Add two cupfuls of sugar rubbed smooth with one cupful of butter.* No, you don't! I know very well that it will taste just the same if the butter is melted, and melted right in the baking pan, so that will be greased at the same time. Have n't I tried it over and over again? *A cupful of milk, and two teaspoonfuls of baking powder.* I shall put everything together and beat them up, with the flour and baking powder added at the last. Five minutes' beating will do just as well as an hour."

This was a specimen of the contests Hope waged with the cook-book, and it must be acknowledged that she generally came off victorious.

The house was clean, and well aired, and reasonably tidy, and homelike. The dishes were always clean and shining. The simple meals were well cooked and daintily served, and flavored with cheer and a sweet temper; and altogether they were about as comfortable as ever were three young people flung on their own resources.

It so happened that this was a season of heavy crops in all parts of the State. If they had possessed a sufficient acreage in bearing fruits, they would have still secured an excellent income, even with the low prices that ruled the market. A few boxes of early cherries sold at an excellent rate, but when they found that apricots and peaches were quoted at but twenty to thirty dollars a ton for the finest qualities, they were discouraged.

"It does n't look as if they would pay for the picking," confessed Ned, in reply to an inquiry from Dr. John. "When we come to pay freight, and cartage, and commission, and reckon on boxes being lost or unsold, — for I hear they find it hard to sell all the fruit that comes in some days of the week, and ours is by no means the first quality, — why, you can see for yourself, Dr. John, it does n't leave any margin."

"Dry them."

"But we have no evaporator, no machine of any kind."

"You need none. In other parts of the world, where rain comes at any or all seasons, it is very necessary to resort to artificial methods. Here, where we are sure of dry, sunny weather throughout the season, there is no necessity for such machines. The markets of the world cannot produce anything to excel our sun-dried California fruits. I am not quite sure that I approve of the sulphuring process; but it not only improves the appearance of the fruit, it is the only process known that effectually protects it from the attacks of insects after it is cured. We have never had an instance of any one being harmed by eating it, and I think, on the whole, I prefer to take my chances on the sulphured fruit, rather than to run the risk of dieting on worms."

Acting on the doctor's advice, the boys procured several bunches of laths and made some fifty trays, three by four feet in dimensions. Upon these they spread their apricots, after first halving and stoning them by one quick pressure of a knife-blade.

A year later they bought a little machine, operated by hand, which did this work in half the time it could be accomplished with a knife; but this year time was plentiful and money scarce with them, and they had to be content with the old-fashioned method. They then placed the trays, in piles of three, upon the ground, and covered them with a tight, box-shaped frame, with a bit of sulphur burning in a hollow on the ground beneath. After twenty minutes' subjection to the fumes, they uncovered the trays and spread them out upon the ground in a sunny spot south of the house, where the fruit cured perfectly in three days, and only needed to be heaped up a day and a night, covered with gunny-sacking, to go through what was called the "sweating process," which had the effect of evenly distributing what little moisture was left in it. After this they tied it up in sacks of plain, unbleached muslin. Their peaches they dried in the same manner, first peeling them by plunging them into a quick bath of scalding lye.

Although this was only the second year's growth of their young orchard, the adventurous little French prunes and the almonds came bravely into bloom, and the former yielded nearly six hundred pounds of fruit. These they dried without stoning, merely giving them a quick dip in the lye they used for peeling the peaches, and another dip into cold water, the object being to cut the skins slightly and hasten the process of drying, thus improving both the appearance and the flavor of the fruit. They found that whereas all of the other fruit lost from four-fifths to six-sevenths of its weight in curing, the French prunes did not lose more than half, and the three hundred pounds of dried fruit contributed by the young orchard formed a welcome addition to their season's crop.

When they came to market it, the entire yield did not bring them any extravagant sum, but it represented a very fair price for the fruit in its fresh state, which they could not have secured that year in any other manner, and they felt that thereafter they should know what to do in a dull season.

The almonds and walnuts in the old orchard helped to swell the season's product, the steady yield of these trees under good treatment, as well as the long age to which they live, being qualities that have brought them into wide popularity. The new orchard yielded only a few handfuls of almonds, and these they took for their own use.

From the vineyard they expected nothing until the third year, knowing that a conservative grapevine takes that space of time to muster its powers of bearing.

They had cultivated the vines faithfully, keeping them free from weeds, and pruned them back, after the conservative plan everywhere practiced with such success. This consisted in keeping the first growth of the vines free from canes, to a height of some ten inches above the ground, so as to form a stout little trunk, then cutting back the abundant growth so as to leave but two or three buds on each branch. Whenever a cane grew in a downward direction or across the path of another, or wherever there were superfluous canes, they were carefully cut away; but late in the spring they were left alone for the season.

Probably no one would have gone near the vineyard again, that season, had it not been for the coyotes.

One night about the middle of September they were awakened by the sound of a light rain falling, an unusual occurrence at that season of the year. At the same time they heard a loud noise from the direction of the chicken house, as of some poor hen in mortal agony.

Dressing themselves hastily they found one of their finest fowls down upon the ground, cackling desperately, with one wing drooping and a large patch of feathers gone from the injured side.

"I know just how it was!" cried Martin in excitement. "She was at the end of the roof, next to the lattice work, when I shut them up. That thing or those things, whatever they are, that have been catching the chickens lately, tried to snatch her."

"You stay here," said Ned, "while I get the lantern. It's just rained enough to moisten the top of the ground, so as to show the creature's tracks. We'll find out what it is and where it's gone."

But when the lantern was brought, and the boys found a track like a large dog's, with the print of four toes plainly marked, they were no nearer the solution than ever.

"Let us see which way it went, anyhow," proposed Martin, catching up the lantern and beginning to examine the ground.

They traced the animal up past the spring, across towards the vineyard, and finally lost the track among the vines. Bending down to search among the trailing canes, Ned found something else.

"Upon my word, Martin, here are — grapes!"

"Pshaw!" said Martin. "Can't be. Grapes never come into bearing until the third year. The Encyclopædia says so."

"Can't help it. Look for yourself. Here are some more — and here — and here! I can feel them where I can't see them."

Martin looked and was convinced. Here, there, and everywhere were grapes. It was a very light crop, it is true, and the bunches were none of them of the great size produced by older vines, but what they lacked collectively, they made up individually, for the single grapes were of unusual size, although there were few bunches that would have weighed more than half a pound.

Early next morning they all went up to the vineyard. The little sprinkle of rain was over, and the day bright and cloudless.

It seemed really surprising that none of them, in passing, had noticed the green and amber bunches hanging amid the clustering leaves. What delight it was to gather them, snipping off the stems with sharp-pointed scissors, laying them warily in the baskets, and even more cautiously into the boxes, that the delicate bloom which makes the beauty of the grape might not be rubbed off.

The young fruit growers were quite exultant over the wonderful yield of their two-year-old vineyard, and anxious to share their experiences with some one else who would publish the news abroad. It so happened that Dr. John, called to a considerable distance by an urgent summons, did not come over, after his usual custom. Instead, Mike McCrary lounged lazily down the trail, accompanied by two dogs, and with his gun upon his shoulder.

"Look here, will you, Mike!" called Martin, as the visitor approached. "You know when we came up here; just two years ago this fall. Well, sir, we set out these vines the spring after that, and see what we're taking off them now!"

"Pretty good show!" said Mike, helping himself to a bunch, but failing entirely in the enthusiasm Martin had expected from him. "Heap of work to put 'em in, and a pile of work to pick 'em!"

"There isn't much of anything worth having that doesn't demand work, I take it," said Ned, gravely.

In spite of themselves, both of the boys could not help liking this good-natured, improvident young fellow; but Ned never let a chance go by to score a point against his way of life.

Mike made no reply. Apparently he was not listening at all, but was watching his dogs, which ran hither and thither, their noses close to the ground, now and then lifting their heads to give an expressive bark and look at their master — or which was the master? In this case Mike promptly acknowledged his subjection.

"What's the matter, Bose? What's up, Fanny? They smell some wild thing," he explained. "Most likely a jack rabbit or a squirrel."

"Perhaps it's the creature that's been carrying off our chickens. It ran off through the vineyard, last night."

"No!" exclaimed Mike, his interest at once awakened. "You seen it?"

"No," said Ned, "but we found its tracks."

"Where be they?" demanded Mike in excitement, starting up at once. "Just let me see them!"

"Right over here is one," said Martin, leading the way to a place he had protected with tall sticks, to keep it from being tramped over.

"Coyote!" pronounced Mike with the air of an oracle, after examining the track. "Did n't you get a pop at it?"

"We have no gun," said Martin.

"Whew! That's too bad," declared the McCrary, with undisguised compassion. "I'd loan you mine, I vum, but how'd I git along without it, say?"

"Oh, we've got the chickens protected now so that they're in no danger," replied Ned. "We have n't time to go hunting, Mike."

"Then I'll loan you my traps," proposed the free-hearted fellow, rather proud, for once, to have something to lend, for two years living in close proximity had developed a very neighborly spirit on the part of the McCrarys.

"I'll be very glad to have them," said Ned, frankly. "Now, Mike, as you have dropped in this afternoon, I have a proposition to make to you. There, Martin, that's the last of the fruit. I'm going to leave you and Hope to get it boxed up, while I go up the hill a ways with Mike."

CHAPTER XXIV.

A PROJECT AND AN ADVENTURE.

Wondering greatly, Mike followed Ned up the steep trail until they reached a point where it commanded a view of the entire hillside.

"This is the north side of the hill," began Ned, "and for two or three hundred yards along here, with the exception of one place, it's all a deep, soft soil. Now suppose, instead of following this steep trail and getting to the top all in a breath and all out of breath, we should cut a road, at an easy grade, along the hill there, and then returning back this way, then taking another turn back there, and then on, over that little knoll, till we reach the thick timber on your quarter-section. It'll be tough work to do it, but it's practicable.

"Now what I've been thinking is this. You want a road out of your place, and we want a way out of ours. To connect with the county road from your place will be a much longer stretch than this, but not so hard, because there are only trees and stones in the way. You take hold and help us with this, and we'll take hold and help you with that. What do you say?"

"I — don't — know," drawled Mike, very conservative, as indolent people always are, about committing himself to any scheme that involved physical exertion. "I'm not sure ef it can be did. How you goin' to git round that ledge of rock that sticks out yonder?"

"Go through it," replied Ned readily. "Giant powder will do the work in no time. I was talking with Dr. John about it yesterday."

"What'd he think about the whole concern?" demanded Mike cautiously.

"He said it could be done. But — shall I tell you exactly what he said?" concluded Ned, desperately.

"Ye–es. Why not?"

"Well, he said I'd never get any of the Mc-Crarys to take hold with me. He said you, Mike, would lounge around the hills all day with your gun, or sit up and watch a rat-hole all night, but that you'd bolt into the next county at the mention of honest work."

Mike's face reddened through its stippling of freckles.

"He said that, did he?" he observed slowly. "Dr. John said that? Well, I'd jest like to knock the doctor out on that statement of his, an' when you git ready to make the road, jest you let me know."

When the young people came to cast up their accounts that fall, they could not help regarding it as a fairly prosperous year, but it must be confessed that it had had its drawbacks. Life, even on a California ranch, is not all composed of red-letter days, and a series of calamities may cast shadows over the sunniest hours.

They had established a colony of cats upon the ranch, for the sole purpose of exterminating the gophers that troubled them, but the latter had nevertheless destroyed the finest of their old fig-trees, while the cats had ravaged birds' nests that Hope had discovered in the spring, and watched with tender interest. The worst of it was that Grimalkin made no distinctions in the bird family, except in favor of the most tender and luscious morsels, and seized upon the young birds whenever she found them plump and juicy, and with not too many feathers to impede feline digestion. So it came to pass that the wrens that built on the kitchen roof, the robins that built in the walnut tree, the swallows that built under the smoke-house eaves, the meadow lark whose nest they had found on the ground in the vineyard, three nests of goldfinches in the peach trees, as well as the woodpeckers in the hollow sycamore down by the brook, all mourned the loss of their offspring, while the linnets, yellow-hammers and blue-jays, most mischievous and destructive of fruit-eating and nut-boring birds, raised their young families in comparative security.

They also mourned the loss of some of their finest poultry, but the handsome skins of two coyotes, tanning by a simple process studied up by the boys, bore witness to the efficacy of Mike McCrary's traps.

The few small bunches of grapes found on the Sultana vines, and the straggling remnant left on the Muscat after the finer ones had been marketed, the young ranchers decided to convert into raisins, and the Encyclopædia taught them how to cure these.

They found that to produce a good raisin it was necessary to let the grapes remain on the vines until they became a rich amber, tinged with brown, showing that the full measure of saccharine matter had found its way into the fruit. To satisfy themselves of the best method of curing, they tried various experiments. They twisted some of the stems, and cut others half-way through with a pen-knife, and left them to cure upon the vines. Some they cut off and laid upon the ground between the vines. Others they hung along cords stretched between the orchard trees. A few were dipped in a weak solution of lye and laid with others, in the natural state, upon the fruit-trays in the sun.

Half of the grapes left hanging on the vines and spread out upon the ground were destroyed by bees and hornets, the latter especially proving most voracious pests, attacking whole bunches and leaving nothing but withered stems and hollow skins. The grapes that were dipped in lye resisted the attacks of insects, but the lye seemed to impart to them a peculiar, candied consistency, which changed the character of the raisin and detracted from its flavor. The bunches hung upon lines, and the grapes spread upon the trays made smaller raisins than those cured upon the ground, but as they had been easily protected by mosquito bar from the ravages of insects, these were voted the most practicable processes to be used in the future.

The young people observed that the "clothesline raisins," as they dubbed those on the lines, cured in less than two-thirds the time required by the others, a very important advantage, in view of the danger of rain during the raisin-curing season.

The California vine-grower and raisin-curer watches sky and clouds, during late October, with as great anxiety and apprehension as ever a New England farmer feels during the haying season.

The part that the Encyclopædia played in life at Home Ranch had its humorous as well as its serious side. They consulted it on every imaginable occasion. Birds and wild flowers were identified by means of it. When caterpillars attacked the trees, and slugs made a raid upon the roses, and galls appeared upon the fruit-tree leaves, and ants swarmed around the drying-trays, the Encyclopædia taught them the remedies. Hope learned from it a trick of making butter come with five minutes' churning, on the warm days when butter did not want to come at all. The boys learned how to graft and bud the fruit-trees successfully, through its illustrated descriptions. In short, it offered generous help in every department of their labor, and one night it averted a most grievous calamity.

That evening Ned had occasion to visit the shed in the corral, where their hay was stored, and returned in great excitement.

"Martin! Hope!" he called, running back towards the house. "Just come over here. I've found the prettiest little squirrel you ever saw. It's striped like a zebra, with black and gold. And it's quite tame. I almost stepped on it before I saw it."

Brother and sister hastened out to join him.

"I'm so glad!" panted Hope. "I've always wanted a tame squirrel. Always, Ned! And you'll make a cage for it, won't you, Martin?"

"Indeed I will," promised Martin; "and one of those turning things to go in it. It will be a nice pet for you, Hope. I'll teach him tricks. Odd about his being so tame, is n't it, Ned? He could n't have got away from anybody and found his way here?"

"I saw him right here, first," explained Ned, for they had come up to the hay-shed. "Had my hands full and could n't pick him up then. He went right over there; almost rubbed against my boot as he passed."

"There he is now. Oh, is n't he a beauty!" exclaimed Martin.

For there, moving slowly around the base of the haystack, was a slender, graceful little animal, with a long pointed nose, bright dark eyes, and an arched back, over which curved an extraordinarily long, bushy tail. Its hair was so long and fine that it looked like a great bunch of thistledown. A black stripe ran down its back, and its sides were dappled with black and amber.

"The dear little thing! I do believe I can catch it with my hands. It does n't look as if it would bite one bit."

"It might, Hope. Better keep on the safe side. I'll throw this sack over it. That's the best way," said Ned, picking up an empty gunny-sack and stealthily advancing upon the pretty creature, while Martin crept behind him, holding up the lantern to guide his way.

"Oh, boys, stop! Don't go a step nearer! I just happened to think — but I've always heard they looked like cats and were black and white. Just wait a minute till I get the Encyclopædia and see if they do have bushy tails. Only think how awful it would be if it should be a ———."

She mentioned the name of a puny little animal held in terror by stalwart men and brave women. At the mere suggestion Ned and Martin showed the white feather and beat an inglorious retreat, tumbling over various implements in their way.

Hope was already half-way to the house. In a few moments she reappeared, carrying a large volume which bore upon the back the inscription: — SHO–TRO.

She knelt down on the earth and turned the leaves with nervous fingers, while Martin looked eagerly over her shoulder, and Ned held the lantern so that its rays would fall upon the book.

"Here it is," she said. "Hold the light a little higher, Ned:—'*Pointed nose — slender and elongated body and a long, bushy tail.*' Oh, it is, it is! '*Walks with back much arched, and the tail erect or curved forward over the body.*' That's just the way it looked. '*Weak, timid, and slow in its movements.*' But no. It can't be, either. This says it is black and white. . . . Oh, here it is:—'*Said to be phosphorescent by night.*'"

"Let us get away from here," said Martin, looking nervously about him. "How do we know where that *Mephitis Mephitica* is prowling now?"

Laughing merrily, they scampered towards the house. On the doorstep Ned pretended to make a critical examination of the fastenings of the door.

"We must double-lock everything to-night," he declared. "But oh, Hope, to think that you were going to adopt for a pet — to catch in your own hands — and Martin was going to make a cage for it and teach tricks to a — a —"

"'Sh!" said Martin. "Call it by its classical name: *Mephitis Mephitica.*"

CHAPTER XXV.

A PREMATURE BLAST.

WHEN Ned and Martin and Mike and his brother Sam had worked for a couple of weeks on the new road, there was not one of them that could have been weaned from the project. Even Sam, who had at first only been held to the task by Mike's covert threats, began to look upon the work he had already done as an investment he could not afford to lose.

By the end of a month they had made grand headway, having reached the projecting ledge beyond which there remained but a few rods more to complete the road up the steep hill.

"I don't see why we must wait for Dr. John to get rid of this big rock. The blasting powder's here, and the drills are here, and all we need is to make some holes and put in the powder," said Mike, as they prepared to go around the ledge and begin work on the other side.

"But you know we don't understand such things, Mike, and there are always accidents occurring in just such ways. I think it's very good of Dr. John to care, and we certainly owe it to him to wait, when he has furnished the powder and the drills."

"Why can't we make the holes with the drills?" urged Mike. "That'll be so much ready when the doctor comes."

Ned readily assented to this scheme, but when the boys had spent half a day at this most difficult labor, without sinking a foot into the hard rock, they were well-nigh discouraged. Mike made a circuit of the ledge and finally climbed on top of it, and in a little time his good-natured face peered over at the boys.

"Say, Ned! Just you go down and ask Dr. John when he'll come up. His buggy's comin' along the road from the station now. Tell him we're clean used up, and you're afraid we'll throw up the whole thing."

Mike waited until he was well out of sight, then beckoned to the younger boys.

"Come along with you, will you, an' see what I've found."

Martin and Sam at once guessed that some important scheme was on hand, and clambered over the ledge in great haste. They found Mike standing over a fissure, which ran completely across the ledge, near its junction with the hill. In the centre of this a wide crevice could be seen, extending down into the heart of the rock.

"Now what's the use of pegging away with thim things," demanded Mike, pointing contemptuously in the direction of the abandoned drills, "whin this big crack's here, riddy to our hand? All we've got to do is, ram the stuff down in here an' touch it off, an' this whole rock 'll go rollin' down the hill like a ball of cotton."

"But are you sure you know how, Mike? Have you ever done it before?" asked Martin, his boy's love of adventure struggling against a sense of obligation to Ned and the doctor.

"Coorse I have. Did n't I stand round day after day when they were workin' on the Mission road, an' blastin' rock by the hunderd ton? An' help 'em, too; I tell you I 'm up to the whole thing. So come on!"

Mike was quite willing to stretch the truth a little, lest he lose prestige with his followers, and he related several exciting anecdotes of experience as he led the way up the hill to the place where the explosives had been stored. By the time they reached there, Martin's misgivings were silenced, and he was disposed to regard Mike as quite a smart fellow after all: much more enterprising than his brother Ned.

But Mike, who had a little superficial knowledge of the use of gunpowder in such cases, had no conception of the dangerous nature of the explosive with which he had to deal. He had some conscience, however, for when he had carried it to the top of the ledge, he ordered the younger boys to stand at a respectful distance, while he faced the risks of his mad prank alone.

A feeling of anxiety gained upon Ned, as he crossed the bridge and walked up through the doctor's grounds.

Dr. John was in the stable, putting up his horse. Ned could hear him speaking kindly to the animal as he secured her in her stall.

"Dr. John!" called Ned.

The doctor came instantly out of the stable.

"Oh, it's you, Ned. Well, what can I do for you?"

"When can you come over to attend to that blasting? I wish you'd come now. I'm afraid — I can't help thinking the boys mean to do something while I'm away."

"Why, what can they do? They can't run away with the road, can they?" asked the doctor good-naturedly.

"No, sir. But the blasting powder —"

"The blasting powder! Did that stupid fellow who brought it here carry it across The Brook?"

The doctor was at once aroused.

"Yes, sir. And we carried it up the hill, so as to have it handy."

"Oh, that is bad, bad!" said the doctor, hastening at once in the direction of The Brook. "And with such a fellow about as that Mike McCrary!"

Dr. John and Ned ran across the hanging bridge and up towards the hill, their apprehension growing with every moment.

Before they reached the old trail there came a deafening roar. An immense mass of rock shot up into the air, and then seemed to separate and rain down in fragments.

Out of the smoke-like cloud of dust that for a moment enveloped the hillside a figure appeared, running swiftly down the road. It was Martin, covered with dirt, and hatless, the blood flowing down one side of his face, where his cheek had been laid bare by a flying fragment of rock.

"I'm all right," he cried breathlessly. "But hurry to the other boys! I'm afraid they're killed. They're making an awful noise."

By this time they could hear a succession of blood-curdling yells, with now and then a low groan like a basso profundo accompaniment.

Ned ran in the direction of the shrieks; the doctor, with true professional instinct, hastened in the direction of the more quiet sufferer. From beneath the projecting shelter of a great boulder Ned hauled Sam McCrary, kicking and screaming, and blanched with fright, but wholly unhurt.

Dr. John's case was more serious. Mike McCrary was lying on his back, where he had evidently been flung by the force of the explosion, the blood trickling over his forehead from an ugly scalp wound, his hands badly torn, and one leg pinioned beneath a heavy stone. Dr. John and Ned lifted this off by their united strength, and then the doctor made a hasty examination.

"A pretty badly mangled leg, and an ugly cut in the head," he announced. "He'll be a very sick fellow before he gets up from this. How to get him home is one problem, and how to get him well in a home like that is another and a harder one."

The doctor was thinking aloud, but the right solution of the difficulty at once flashed across Ned. Mike ought not be jarred or carried any further than possible. Yet how could they stand it, to take this great, coarse, dirty fellow into their neat little home?

Of course the Good Samaritan would not have hesitated; but then the Good Samaritan helped people by the wayside; he did n't take them to his home.

"Dr. John," said Ned quietly, "we will carry him down to our house."

"Very well," said the doctor just as quietly, never hinting that he had divined the struggle through which the boy had been passing.

They brought up the drag the boys used on the place, and with great difficulty got Mike down to the cottage, where he was laid on the boys' own bed.

For a couple of weeks Mike had a high fever and required constant attention, but when he grew better he seemed to fret so much over the failure of their project and his own helplessness, that the boys returned to their work upon the road, and were joined by Sam, who was very much subdued, and showed himself amenable to orders from that time forth.

The accident had occurred about the middle of October, and by the middle of November they had reached the brow of the hill and commenced to blaze their way through the dense growth of timber above. When they had got partly through the

McCrary place, some of the neighbors, knowing of Mike's misfortune, volunteered to complete the road, offering to take their pay in the wood that was cut down in clearing it.

It was well into November when Mike was sufficiently recovered to attempt his journey home.

"Do you feel quite able to go, Mike?" asked Ned, kindly. He could not help being secretly relieved at the departure of this uncongenial guest, but he was all the more determined not to be remiss in any of the dues of hospitality.

"Yes, I'm able, so far as that goes, but I'll be blessed if I want to," confessed Mike frankly. "Boys, I know I've been a trouble to you, an' in the way, an' it hasn't been just like home to you with a big, rough fellow like me lyin' around."

"Oh, no!" "Not at all!" the boys hastened to say, but Mike persisted: —

"Yes, it's been a bother, an' you know it, an' I know it. An' your sister — little lady as she is — knows it. Do you s'pose I didn't know it went agin the grain to have me eatin' an' drinkin' out of her nice dishes an' settin' round her tidy rooms, not knowin' so much as how to do it genteelly, neither? But I tell you, boys, it seems 's if I niver lived before. You know what I've got to go back to."

The boys hardly knew what to say to this outburst of confidence. Mike relieved them of all embarrassment by cutting short the conversation himself.

"Well, I must be goin'," he said. "Thank you

kindly for what you've done for me. After all, a man's bed is what he makes it. P'r'aps I might be makin' mine better when I git about agin."

It was several weeks more before Mike McCrary's budding ambition found a chance to expand. Early one morning, Dr. John, going down to his stable to harness his horse, met Mike, still a little pale, and limping slightly.

"Dr. John," he said modestly, "will you loan me a hoe for a week or so?"

"Certainly, Mike. There are plenty here in the tool-house. Help yourself."

Mike selected one that was broad and heavy.

"I 'm goin' to try to git work down to Abbott's nursery," he exclaimed. "A man was tellin' me they 're short of hands in hoein'."

"Then jump into the buggy and I 'll give you a lift. I have to go by there this morning," said Dr. John.

On the road Mike was speechless for a time; then he broke the silence by saying: —

"It was too much for me, doctor, when I got back there."

He pointed over the hills in the direction of his home.

"At the Austins', it was different like, you know."

"Enterprising young people!" commented the doctor. "Do you know what they are busy about now?"

"No, sir."

"Putting a hydraulic ram in The Brook to increase their supply of water, so that they can irrigate the lower part of their place. They found that a few old fig-trees were paying better than anything else on their ranch, so they encouraged the growth of a lot of suckers, and when the wet season had fairly set in, they planted them out. There are a hundred or more of them, and they will commence bearing a year and a half from now. The only drawback was the lack of a copious supply of water. This is their way of meeting it."

But Mike, with the pertinacity of people of his kind, was not to be diverted from his subject.

"I could n't stand it after I got home. You knew about my father, doctor?"

"I have heard — something," replied the Doctor, conservatively.

"Then you know. He hung himself. I think if he 'd just plucked up and fought it out, it 'd a been better for us. My mother — is a different sort."

He broke off abruptly for a moment, than resumed.

"We 've got plenty of land there, — good land, too; but not a red cent to cultivate it. We 've lived from hand to mouth all along. Let the cattle take care of themselves, and sold a calf or cow or a horse to pay the storekeepers, — when they were paid! It 's goin' to be different now. I 'm goin' to make a raise."

Dr. John gave a keen, sidelong glance at his

companion. Was this Mike McCrary, the idle, worthless fellow, whom he had held in contempt for years? Would this newly conceived ambition hold out?

As Mike got out of the buggy he turned to Dr. John with some of his old roguery.

"I come pretty nigh 'boltin' into the next county,' but it was n't to dodge the work on the road, doctor. An' you 'll surely own that my blast cleared the road, sir, if it did clear a good deal else along with it."

CHAPTER XXVI.

THE BUILDING OF THE BRIDGE.

EARLY one morning in the following spring, Dr. John appeared at Home Ranch with a look of quiet satisfaction on his face.

"Well, young folks, I have some agreeable news for you," he announced. "The county supervisors have decided to build a bridge across The Brook, to connect with your new road."

"You don't say so!" cried Martin.

"What ever started them? How did they know about the road?" asked Ned.

"Oh, they heard of it some way or other," replied the doctor, calmly. "It makes a short cut to the next town up in the mountains."

"It will be an immense advantage to us. It will give us a chance to get help when we need it, for one thing. We can do a good many things that we can't do now without help. Catch a Chinaman trusting himself to our suspension bridge!" remarked Ned.

"Yes, it will be an advantage to you, on the whole, I think," replied the doctor.

No one could have suspected from Dr. John's careless manner that he had been first and foremost in promoting the entire scheme. He had first laid the matter before the supervisor from their township, who had introduced the proposition in open board. When it appeared that the rest of the body were inclined to take but a lukewarm interest in the matter, Dr. John had not been discouraged. He had addressed a communication to the supervisors, setting forth, in clear language, the saving of time and travel that would accrue from connecting with the new road, and had asked, in a forcible way, whether the supervisors of Alameda County had not sufficient energy and enterprise to match the efforts of a parcel of boys. This letter he had backed up by a petition, signed by all the people of substance throughout the valley, asking that the bridge should be built, and the Board had yielded a tardy surrender to the logic of circumstances.

"Of course the building of the bridge implies the laying out of a public road through both of our places," explained the doctor. "The ground will be condemned and paid for at a reasonable rate. We must take pains to have it pass along the side of Home Ranch, so as not to cut the place in two. It is going to make a difference to you in more than one way. Soon the great outside world — the world that is afraid of quicksands and swinging bridges — will be crowding in upon you. Don't let it come too near."

The boys were busy with their spring plowing, and knowing that Dr. John never permitted them to make any difference in their work when he was there, having finished their breakfast, they went out.

Hope, who had bread to bake, stepped into the pantry, pulled out her cakeboard and commenced to knead the dough she had mixed while waiting for the boys to come in to breakfast. She was very quiet, thinking over Dr. John's last words, which seemed to her to hold a deep significance.

The doctor was quiet, too, and he was thinking about Hope. He had become attached to the young girl, during the two years and more that they had lived in such close neighborship, but he had to confess to himself that she puzzled him. He was accustomed to the ordinary type of girl, bright, talkative, plucky, ambitious, eager to take a position in the world. This shy little body, who went so quietly about her self-appointed tasks, who never expressed any desire to mingle with other girls of her age, who knew no amusements beyond the daily happenings on the ranch, was a new type to him.

"Hope," he said, gently; "don't you care anything for dress?"

The girl looked up, surprised by his tone and inquiry.

"For pretty clothes, such as girls usually fancy," he explained smilingly. "For silks, and laces, and beautiful jewels, such as women of fashion wear."

It was not a new thought to Hope. He could see that by the expression of her face. So the girl had her temptations and weaknesses to camp down, silently and uncomplainingly as she fought her battles.

"I might," she answered frankly, "if other things made it right. Sometimes I think that this life is good for me in that very way. If I had been able to have all those things, I am afraid I should have thought of little else. I should have been a selfish little peacock, and the boys — the boys would have despised me."

She drew a long breath and gave the lump of dough she was kneading some very unnecessary thumps, as if it represented the frivolous spirit she had found it so hard to conquer. Perhaps the thought came into her mind that if she could have had all the pretty things her girlish fancy craved, she could have borne very well to be despised by the boys.

"It does n't trouble me one bit to go without them," she insisted bravely; "but there is one thing I should like: to be dressed perfectly, all through, just for once. I think I should like brown best," she continued, speculatively, tipping her little head to one side and absently holding up a lump of dough that she had separated from the rest, to make into a loaf. "A pretty, dark brown wool dress, the very finest and costliest material, but wool; and a brown jacket, and a brown hat, and brown gloves, and — yes, some bronze boots. Everything the very best of its kind. Not for people to see. For my own comfort, even if I only put them on once in a great while and took a little walk, all by myself, about the ranch. Oh, I know it's perfectly absurd," she concluded, with a little bird-like laugh.

But Dr. John did not appear to be listening at all, and Hope felt quite rebuked for her levity. He was making an entry in a little note-book he carried in his pocket. When he had replaced it he took his leave, but Hope's cheeks burned for an hour afterwards, over the recollection of her folly.

They who plant fruit-trees in California do not plant for coming generations. Mother Nature is bountiful in the Golden State, and hastens to reward those who serve her.

The third year, the occupants of Home Ranch commenced to reap a substantial return for their labors. They now had six acres of orchard fruit in bearing, and each succeeding year would increase the product. In addition to this, they had seven acres of young orchard, including the figs, and had added three acres to their vineyard, using cuttings from their own vines.

They had reached the point of an assured prosperity, and knew that with economy they could meet any ordinary emergency, while their income was sure to increase steadily, year after year. They still kept up their studies, and hoped another year to be able to lighten their labors, now growing a little too heavy for them, by hiring extra help in the fruit season.

The few strangers with whom they came in contact from time to time remarked their unusual intelligence and breadth of substantial knowledge, but there was a certain quaint precision of speech, an excess of earnestness of manner, which is very sure to mark those who live apart, and whose intellectual training has been almost wholly acquired from books.

It was not until late in August that the bridge was built, but when it was at length completed they found the doctor's prediction verified.

The world — the little world of the valley — rushed in upon them. The boys, accustomed to meet the men of the community, as well as boys of their own age, on their frequent trips to the village, were little discomposed by the change, although it was observable that Martin grew particular about his toilet, and never went out or came in without stealing a look in the glass to make sure that his hair was neatly brushed and his face clean. Ned took a hearty pleasure in the visits of other young farmers and farmers' sons, and took them about the place to look at the trees and vines, or discussed various modes of culture with them, with great satisfaction.

With Hope, now a tall, fair girl of fourteen, it was wholly different. She could not reconcile herself all at once to this invasion of their privacy. The whole world seemed to have been turned topsy-turvy. She trembled at the sound of carriage-wheels more than she had ever faltered at the shock of a California earthquake, and was conscious at times of a barbarous wish that the bridge might be consumed by fire or swept away by a freshet. She had always been painfully shy, and to suddenly become the mark of so much social attention was almost more than she could bear.

"Oh, I wish they would stop it, or would n't come at all," she once said in an undertone to Ned, after a carriage-load of callers had rolled away.

"Stop what?" asked Ned in surprise.

"Don't you see how the ladies — the middle-aged ones — all look on me with compassion, as if I were just rescued from some long and terrible exile? They talk to me as if they were missionaries, and I a forlorn little pagan. And the young ladies — I don't dare call them girls — act as if I were some wild animal escaped from a menagerie."

Hope did not realize that her own unusual dignity, which masked her natural timidity, and her seriousness, overawed the young people of her own age. She saw them look curiously at her, and became conscious that her clothes were old-fashioned and plain. She observed that they hesitated while talking with her, and thought that she had tired them with her dullness. She resented the insinuation that her years of separation and seclusion had been years of martyrdom: those happy, useful years. The only sorrow she had was one she could not bare to the casual comments of strangers: the thought of her father, sick, helpless and lonely, chained down by disease.

Occasionally city people came across the bridge

and up the road, bound on merry jaunts across the range.

One day a party of young men, rigged out for a hunt, and driving a team of fast horses, came up the road. They were a wild and noisy crowd. All of them had cigars in their mouths, and they had evidently been drinking. Hope was at work among her roses as she saw them coming, and she wondered when they drew up at the gate of Home Ranch.

"Here's for a raid on that vineyard!" she heard one of them shout, as he led the way for the rest to follow.

"I see something better: a lot of roses and a pretty girl. Here's for a kiss!" sang out another's merry voice, and she saw him leave his companions and come down towards her, while the others halted and looked after him, as if uncertain whether to keep on or to follow him.

Hope turned away from him, but she stood her ground and busied herself with her roses, confronting him with a pale face and flashing eyes, as she heard his step behind her.

It is difficult to say which of the two was most shocked and abashed.

"Oh, Tom Bateman!" cried Hope.

"Hope Austin!" was all that Tom could stammer at first, but he threw away the cigar he was smoking.

"I'm sorry, Hope. Indeed, I meant nothing by it. We're out on a regular lark, — but this is the worst thing I've done. Indeed it is! I'm heartily ashamed of myself."

"Go!" said Hope severely, pointing to the gate and to the young fellows who were waiting. "Go! And I hope, Tom Bateman, I'll never see you again as long as I live, if it has to be like this."

Without a word, he did as she bade him, and would have taken his companions with him, but at that moment the boys appeared, coming in to luncheon. They hailed him cordially.

"Why, how are you, Tom? Come to make us a little visit, I hope," said Ned.

"Not to-day," replied Tom, greatly embarrassed. "To tell you the truth, I did n't know you lived here. It was quite by accident we stopped at all."

"Oh, but you ought to come up and see Beauty," urged Martin. "She's the prettiest cow in all the valley. Every one admires her. Her calf is almost as large as she is now."

"I — I can't stop!" insisted Tom, taking a step towards the road, where the rest of the party were already climbing into their cart. "You've got a neat little place up here. I suppose you fellows have no end of fun, driving about the country, and hunting, and fishing, and such things."

"We have plenty of fun," returned Ned, pleasantly, "but not precisely that kind. We don't have much time to seek our own pleasure, so we find pleasure in our work and duty."

"Really?" said Tom, with honest sympathy.

"Oh, you mus'n't pity us. We would n't change

places with the jolliest of you city fellows. Come up and try it yourself."

"Another time!" said Tom.

"All right. Another time," rejoined the boys; but they both wondered whether Tom would keep his word.

The rest of the trip was spoiled for Tom. Wherever they went, and in all their frolics, he saw continually before him an earnest little face looking with contempt upon him, and heard a sweet, girlish voice, saying:—

"I hope I'll never see you again, if it's to be like this."

As for Hope, she went sadly up to the house, saying over and over again to herself:—

"Oh, I wish the bridge had never been built. I wish it had never been built."

Yet the bridge was to give them many a lift on the road to a greater prosperity, and to bring great happiness to them.

CHAPTER XXVII.

A PRISONER OF WAR.

THE building of the bridge brought its train of disaster, as well as its benefits.

One Saturday afternoon, late in November, soon after its completion, Hope was seated in her little rocking-chair just outside the door, darning stockings and humming a little song to herself, while the boys were pruning in the vineyard.

Down the road she saw some one coming. A tall, burly man had crossed the bridge, and was coming up the road. Now and then he stopped and surveyed the place.

Had any one been near enough to see, they might have wondered at the cunning look of gratification that overspread his face. Not a thing escaped his eye: the thriving hedge planted along the road; the vigorous orchard; the ground beneath the trees, destitute of a weed or spear of grass; the vineyard, carefully staked out and with the vines already pruned; the long rows of roses, now luxurious with bloom.

As he turned into the place and lounged around so as to obtain a closer view of the house, which now looked " as if it belonged to somebody," as the doctor had said, a broad grin of delight, not unmixed with surprise, overspread the fellow's face. He noted the newly shingled roof, the screens at doors and windows, the shelf outside of the back door, with its row of glittering milk-pans shining in the sun, the flower-beds around the house, the general air of thrift and comfort. Not a detail escaped his eye.

"Well, I vum!" he said.

He strolled around to the front of the house, and came suddenly upon Hope, in her neat gingham dress, with the sunshine sifting down through the pepper-trees upon her head, touching her brown hair with golden glints. She wore a plain linen collar and had a bright bow of ribbon at her throat, and was altogether as fair and sweet a vision of dawning womanhood as one often sees.

A coarse oath fell from the man's lips at the sight.

"——it! Thought I'd got only a passel o' boys to deal with. Bother the wimmen folks!"

Hope gave a little start at the unexpected appearance of the stranger and his muttered exclamation, and sprang up from her seat.

"Did you — do you want to see anybody? I thought you had gone up the orchard to the boys."

She had little knowledge of the world, but the bleared eyes, the brutish mouth, the red swollen face of this man possessed her with an instinctive dread.

Her agitation reassured the fellow.

"Reckon I do," he said roughly. "Reckon I've suthin' to say to them boys — yo' brothers, be they?"

Hope drew from her pocket a small hunting-whistle, one that the boys had once given her to call them to their meals when they were out of hearing. She placed this to her mouth and blew a shrill summons upon it. Up the cañon the echoes answered her, and a mocking call came from the rough crags of the hillside back of the place, blending with the boys' voices, as they united in a hearty response.

Her heart gave a bound when she heard the sound of the boys' hurrying feet, and a moment later they came into sight.

Ned wore a loose flannel blouse, unbuttoned at the neck and showing his white, girlish throat. An old straw hat was on his head, and in his hand he carried a pair of heavy pruning shears. Martin followed, wearing a loose jumper and overalls. The faces of both boys were flushed by running. They were sure something unusual had occurred, or Hope would never have blown the whistle.

The burly visitor looked at them in evident satisfaction. They were fine specimens of American boyhood, brave, manly young fellows, every inch of them; but they were by no means men, according to his standard.

"How old be yo'?"

He put the question to Ned, who had been waiting

in silence for him to make known his errand. There was something so sinister about the man's face and manner that Ned hesitated an instant before replying. Then he answered quietly: —

"Eighteen last July."

"Reckoned yo' was n't beyant it. An' how long be yo' heah?"

"Three years in September."

"Filed on 't? Gov'ment land, hey?" persevered the visitor.

"I did. What business is it of yours?" demanded Ned, nettled by the impertinent questions and jeering tone.

The stranger viewed him with the cruel eye a cold-blooded angler bends on the little fish that has swallowed his bait, and which he plays awhile before jerking out of the water.

"Le' 's go in the house," he said. "Reckon I 'd like to look around a bit."

This was decidedly too much: to have their little home invaded by this impertinent trespasser, who had already frightened Hope and called them from their work, robbing them of precious time! Ned placed himself before the door and looked up boldly into the stranger's face.

"Out of the way, blast yo', yo' young scoundrel!" growled the man, seizing Ned by the shoulder and attempting to shove him roughly aside, when a new actor appeared on the scene.

Old Tray, fast drifting into the lethargy of age, appeared inside of the screen door, his great body poised as if for a spring, his eyes gleaming with a fierce light, and his great teeth parted in a low growl.

The man gazed at the dog with a look of horror. His ugly grasp of Ned's shoulder changed to a movement of appeal. He fell back a little, pulling the boy a little nearer the door.

"Look thar!" he said in an awed voice.

"Well?" said Ned carelessly, glancing up with contempt at the big fellow who could be alarmed at the sight of a dog.

"Tell me, pon honah! Don't yo' see nothin' thar?"

Something moved Ned, always a truthful boy, to fly directly in the face of fact.

"Of course I don't," he replied carelessly. "What should I see?"

"Don't see nothin' that looks like a dog, — a big black dog, suthin' the matter with one hind leg,— his eyes like bloody vengeance, — ready to tear the man to pieces as did it?"

"Certainly not!" said Ned.

"Got 'em agin!" muttered the man, falling back and retreating cautiously to a vantage ground under the pepper-trees, whence he looked about him apprehensively, as if expecting to meet everywhere the phantom born of a guilty conscience.

They were beginning to understand. It did not surprise them greatly when he recovered his bullying air and renewed his abusive talk.

"I'd like to know who's got a bettah right to

this heah 'dobe than the man that built it. You want to know who I be? I'm Hank Jones. An' what 'm I doin' heah? I 'm come to claim my prop'ty."

He laughed coarsely and went on.

"Got things fixed up right smart, ain't yo'? Much 'bliged to yo', I 'm sho'. I 'll not be hard on yo'. Some folks 'd chahge yo' back rent. I 'm not that small. Take time to pack up yo' traps, an' be off. No 'bjection ef yo' want to stay till mo'nin'. Reckon I 'll take a look ovah the ranch, an' see ef it 's fahmed to my likin'."

He swaggered off around the house as he concluded, while the brothers and sister looked at each other in dismay. What they had heard, coarsely and roughly as it was expressed, came to them with an awful conviction of its truth.

They would have to give up the little home they had toiled so long to secure, and which they had worked so cheerfully to make comfortable and attractive.

"Oh, Ned, I 'd rather die!" moaned Hope.

"Let 's kill him!" said Martin fiercely.

"Hush!" said Ned. He was busy thinking, but no happy inspiration came to his relief. Instead, he remembered the schoolmaster's misgivings, the reluctance of the employees of the Land Office, the hesitating encouragement of the Surveyor General on the day they had first proposed entering the land.

They had not the means to make a legal contest.

Even if they had, it was not probable they would have any show of winning it.

They sat down together on a seat beneath the larger of the pepper-trees. There seemed nothing left for them but submission.

A couple of hours passed by, and the sun sunk low in the west, its level rays illuminating all the place. The children looked sadly about at the glories of the sunset sky and the gilded beauty of the hills, wondering if it was the last time they would ever see a sunset there. The boys forgot that they were hungry, forgot that their hard day's work called for refreshment and repose. Hope, usually so thoughtful for others, was blind to everything but the thought that they were about to leave their little home and be cast adrift upon the world again.

At last they saw a large figure moving through the shrubbery, and drew a little nearer together as they recognized the stranger: the man who had announced himself as Hank Jones, and who had come to seize the ranch.

The demands of the animal, in big, coarse fellows like this Missouri giant, outweigh the strength of the spirit, and even foil their own vicious schemes.

Hank Jones was hungry. Hunger made him more complaisant. A few hours before he would not have parted with his claim on the ranch at any price. Now, he was ready to abate it.

"Now, lookee heah, young uns," he began, in

what he intended for a conciliatory tone. "Yo' uns all know what minors means?"

"Certainly," said Ned.

"An' bein' minors, yo' ain't got no shadow o' a show in any coht o' law."

The young people were speechless.

"Now, yo' see I got the dead drop on yo', so fah 's the title to this heah prop'ty 's consehned?"

"Did you ever prove upon it?" asked Ned, sharply.

"Don't yo' be too smaht!" admonished Hank Jones sourly, eying the boy with a malevolent look. "I 've proved up a heap mo 'n yo 'll evah do. I broke the first land heah; I put up that 'dobe yon. I 've done a sight mo 'n them rich land-grabbers evah do. I 'm a M'ssou'y gen'leman, I am, 'n' I can sweah my way through any coht, slick 's lightnin', 'n' don't yo' fohget it! But what I 's 'bout to say 's this: Ef yo' want to buy me off, I 'm fo' sale. My figgah 's jes ten thousand dollahs."

"But we hav n't any money —" began Ned.

Hope put her hand gently over his mouth. The spirit of her revolutionary grandmothers flashed up in her.

"Don't talk to him. I would n't buy him off if we had a hundred thousand. I don't believe he has any right to the place. I don't believe the courts would help on such injustice."

The big Missourian looked at her with secret admiration.

"She 's a 'tarnal tongue for a gal!" he said

aloud. "Don't le' 's jaw any mo' 'bout the business this evenin'. Mought be we could fix it up tomorrah. Reckon yo' got some friends what 'll loan the stamps. Hain't got a side o' bacon hangin' round heah, somewhar? Durned ef I don't see what grub thar is on this ranch!"

Body had the ascendancy now. Hank Jones would not press his claim further until he had something to eat. It occurred to Ned that it might be well, as a matter of policy, to feed their tormentor. He looked at Hope, but Hope pressed her lips tightly together and shook her head. The little housewife thought of her store of good things in the pantry — her Saturday's baking of custard pies and tarts and brownbread — and trembled for them if this huge gourmand should come across them.

Seeing that the broad hint he had given brought no response, Hank Jones started off to forage for himself.

"If we could only get him out of the way till we got our spring crops in, we 'd have something to fight with," said Ned, gloomily.

The boys were standing in characteristic attitudes, Ned with his hands in his pockets, a scowl on his forehead, and a look of deep perplexity in his eyes; Martin leaning against a tree and whistling a melancholy tune.

Hope, concerned for her pantry and the good things in it, dropped upon her knees and peered under the low branches of the trees, the better to observe the actions of the visitor. He was nearing the rear corner of the house. He was stopping, and looking in the direction of the kitchen. He was going in! No, he had changed his mind and was striking off across the garden. Where could he be bound now? Ah, she saw!

When the Missourian had squatted on the land, years before, as soon as he had a roof over his head and before he thought of providing any shelter for his stock, in fact before he so much as made a kitchen, he had been true to Southern traditions and put up a smokehouse.

This smokehouse was more suggestive of a stockade for purposes of border warfare or defense than of the innocent purposes for which it was designed. In the scarcity of mill lumber, it had been constructed of massive, rough-hewn logs. It was destitute of windows, its only opening being a stout but clumsy door in front.

To secure his smoked meats against depredation, the builder had attached a heavy iron hasp and staple to door and building, and hanging from the latter was a rusty padlock, long disused, picked up and hung there by Dr. John, when they first looked at the building. Ned had utilized this smokehouse for storing his box material, and there was nothing in it but a few bundles of shooks and some empty boxes.

It was towards this building that the Missourian, drawn by the charm of old associations, had bent his steps. "He's going in," said Hope, in a low voice thrilling with excitement. "He's going in!

No, he isn't. Oh dear! He's turning away. No, he's put his head in, he is going in —"

"What in the creation is the matter, Hope?" "What do you mean, Hope?" exclaimed both boys in a breath.

"*He's in!*" cried the girl, and without another word she flew like a deer through the shrubbery and across the garden, swung the door upon the luckless forager, caught the padlock, slipped the hasp into place and the arm of the padlock through the staple, springing it shut with all the force of her small hands. Not content with this, she darted to a pile of timbers near by, and had dragged out a stout piece and was bracing it against the door when the boys came up. They took in the situation at a glance.

"Good for you, Hope!" said Ned, beneath his breath, while Martin clapped his hands and shouted in an ecstasy of delight.

"Le' me out!"

The slow-witted Missourian had stopped rummaging among the boxes and shook the door fiercely before he realized the situation.

The only answer to the prisoner's demand was a fresh peal of laughter from Martin.

"Le' me out or I'll kick the dog-goned place all to slivers!"

"Come now, boys!" said the prisoner persuasively. "Quit yo' foolin' an' le' me out."

"Shan't do it!" said Martin, saucily.

"It's a good joke, boys. A 'tarnal good joke,"

said the Missourian from behind his bars. "But it's gittin' late. I ain't had a bite sence mawnin'. Le' me out an' I'll call it quits."

"Will you give up your claim on the ranch?" asked Ned, in a business-like tone.

"Not much I don't. Oh, yo' young rascals! I'll lick yo' for this when I git out o' heah."

But he had the empty air for an audience. Ned had caught up the milk-pail and was off to the cow. Hope had run down to attend her little chickens, and Martin was kindling a fire in the kitchen stove.

CHAPTER XXVIII.

HOW HANK JONES'S CLAIM WAS SETTLED.

TEN days later Dr. John, starting for an after-dinner walk across The Brook, saw Ned walking slowly towards him upon the bridge, his head hanging in a dejected manner, while he absently tore the bark from a long willow switch that he carried.

"Something is the matter with those children," said Dr. John to himself, "and I shan't rest another night until I find out what it is."

Since the bridge had been built and the world had rushed in upon Home Ranch, Dr. John had ceased to go there as frequently as before. His interest in the young people, however, was as strong as ever, and for several days he had noticed that they held themselves strangely aloof. Walking down to the station, the previous Sunday, he had come upon Martin, on his way alone to the Sunday School in the village. When the doctor had inquired why the others were not along, as usual, the young fellow had reddened and stammered an evasive reply.

"Something's certainly wrong!" reflected the doctor. "I only hope they have n't quarreled among themselves."

"Well, Ned?" he said heartily. "How are things going on up at the ranch?"

"Pretty well, I thank you, sir," replied Ned. Then he was overpowered by the sense of the falsehood he was uttering.

"Not exactly that, either. Things are not going well at all, Dr. John. In fact, they're going about as badly as they could," he said desperately, resolved to make a clean breast of the whole matter and take counsel with the doctor.

"Why, how is this, my boy? Gophers eating the roots of the young fig-trees, raccoons after the chickens, or the cow got the colic? Out with it, whatever it is!"

"Dr. John," said Ned piteously, disregarding the bantering tone, "did you ever know Hank Jones, the man who first entered on our land?"

"Know him? Yes," replied the doctor, a quizzical smile dwelling on his face for a moment. "He used to hang about the village before he tried farming. I can't say that we were ever formally introduced, but I once made his acquaintance over my hen-roost, after dark."

"Oh, is he that kind of a man?" exclaimed Ned. "Well, he came up here a week ago last Saturday. He says we have no right to file on the land, being minors with a parent living. He says he has a better right to the land than we. He says he can prove it in the court. He told us to pack up our things and be off."

"My patience!" said the doctor, who evidently

had very little patience to spare, on receiving this intelligence. "Why didn't you call me over? Don't worry your heads over such a preposterous claim. Have you heard anything from him since?"

"Why — well — you see — the truth is," stammered Ned, "he did n't go off. He's up there still."

"Up there still!" repeated the doctor wrathfully. "You don't mean to say he's taken possession?"

"N — no!" returned Ned timidly. "He has n't exactly taken possession. In fact, it's rather the other way. We — have taken possession — of him."

"What!" exploded the doctor, turning around and facing the boy.

"We — captured him. Or rather Hope did. She's got him in the smokehouse."

Ned wound up with a hysterical chuckle.

"Ned Austin, are you crazy? The Hank Jones I am talking of is a giant of a man, six feet and a half high and weighing at least two hundred and seventy-five pounds."

"I know it," gasped Ned, "but we've got him. And Hope did it. He was prowling about, trying to find something to eat. He went into the smokehouse. Hope saw him and slipped up and fastened him in. He's been there ten days."

"Hold on, Ned! I can't stand any more. Ha, ha, ha, ha, ha, ha!"

The hills echoed and reëchoed the hearty peals

of laughter. An old blue heron, alarmed by the sound, left her nest in the tall sycamore above them, and soared up the cañon. Ned eyed the doctor resentfully.

"It's no laughing matter to us," he said, "I did n't think you 'd make fun of us."

"Big Hank Jones jailed by little Hope! That great braggart taken prisoner by a slight, fourteen-year-old girl!" laughed Dr. John. "But what are you going to do with him?"

"That's just the trouble, doctor," replied the boy gravely. "We don't quite know. We thought if we could only keep him out of the way till we got this spring's crop in and some money to hire a lawyer, — but he makes such a fuss: such an awful noise. We 've been on nettles for fear somebody would come to see us and hear him. This afternoon he 's been more quiet. I 'm afraid the smokehouse is n't healthy. I think he 's getting weaker."

"Very possible. It is n't exactly conducive to strength to fast for ten days running."

"Oh, we 've fed him," Ned hastened to explain, "through a chink in the wall. Martin was for giving him nothing but cornmeal and water, — the same we feed the little chickens; thought it would break him down quickest. But I insisted on bread and water; only Hope will butter the bread and throw in a piece of pie once a day. I 've given him every chance to do the right thing. Twice a day, regularly, I 've gone there and asked him how much he 'd take for his claim."

"And what did he say?"

"At first he swore he wouldn't take a penny less than ten thousand dollars. But he's dropped since. This morning he came down to a thousand. He's awful hungry," concluded Ned confidentially.

"Now you're laughing again, Dr. John," he added reproachfully.

"Ned, I protest I was never more serious in my life," asserted the doctor, but a mirthful gleam in his eye and a little break in his voice contradicted his solemn statement.

"Suppose I go up and interview this — this prisoner of yours."

"If you only would!" cried the boy. It seemed a little cowardly, but it was altogether comfortable, to shift this heavy burden to Dr. John's shoulders.

Ned made just one more remark, on the way up to the house: —

"It's an awful responsibility to be the head of a family."

The doctor's eyes twinkled again at the sight of Hope's guilty start as she came out of the chickenyard and saw him. As they approached the house, the reason for Ned's solicitude became manifest.

A series of unearthly groans, howls and fierce invectives, accompanied by the sound of lusty kicks, were heard in the direction of the smokehouse.

As they turned the corner of the house they came upon Martin, mounting guard on an old sawhorse. He dismounted and came toward the doctor, who smiled at his careworn look.

At the sound of footsteps the commotion in the smokehouse subsided, only to be renewed in a different key.

"Help! Help! Muhdah! Le' me out o' heah! Them little beggahs locked me up. I'm the rightful ownah this ranch!"

"He might take a notion to burrow out," explained Ned in a troubled whisper.

"Ask him how much he'll take now to make peace," suggested Dr. John.

"How much will you take to settle your claim against the ranch, Mr. Jones?" said Ned in a business-like tone.

There was a moment's silence, as if the prisoner was meditating.

"Five hundred dollars," came the weak reply. "Yo' can sholy borry the money from somebody. Thar's Dr. John, now. Jest ast him. Thar's no need of tellin' him what it's fo'. Tell him yo' 'low yo' got in a tight place, an' that'll help yo' out. He'll take pleazhah in 'commodaten' o' yo'."

"I guess you'll take less than that, Hank Jones," said the doctor coolly. "Suppose you settle for a ticket back to the city, and a good kicking."

"Thundah!" came the startled response from the interior of the smokehouse. Hank Jones recognized the doctor's voice, and knew that his game was up.

The doctor turned the key in the padlock and the door swung wide, disclosing the captive sitting in a disconsolate attitude on the floor. His liberator seized him by the collar and jerked him out, administering the promised kick as he did so.

"Take that, you lazy hulk of a fellow!" said Dr. John. "The next time you want to browbeat any one into pensioning off an idle vagabond, let it be a man of your own size, and not a household of honest, industrious children. If ever you show yourself in this locality again, I have an account of my own to settle with you, and I promise you a short shrift."

Ned and Martin and Hope beheld the discomfiture of their enemy in surprise, and not without a sense of amusement.

As big Hank turned to go, he caught sight of Martin's beaming face, and shook his fist menacingly at the boy.

"Nevah yo' mind, yo' little rascal! Yo'll nevah play no mo' monkey shines on me. I'll have the law on yo' yet. Yo's the ornariest, mischievousest, good fo' nothin'" —

His anathema was interrupted in an unexpected fashion. Hope took a step forward, put her hand on Martin's shoulder, and looking Mr. Jones full in the face, said quietly: —

"I did it."

"Yo'?" The Missourian stopped short and surveyed the little girl like a man in a dream.

"Yes," said Hope simply.

A look of unmistakable admiration came into the rowdy's face.

"Well, I vum!"

With this exclamation, he turned on his heel, and Home Ranch saw him no more.

After the prisoner had taken his leave it was the children who were merry and light-hearted, the doctor who was troubled and thoughtful.

"I wonder if we ought not, in justice, pay him for the improvements on the place," said Ned, when their laughter had subsided. "He built them, and we certainly have the benefit of them."

"Don't trouble yourself with the thought of any such obligation," contended Dr. John warmly. "He left them behind him, simply because he could n't carry them away or sell them. Some day when you are able, make up for them by giving help to some poor family in the valley, ruined by the corrupt influences of Hank Jones and his drunken, gambling set."

"That's a good idea," said Ned. "I confess, Dr. John, the man really impressed me with the weakness of our claim upon the ranch. Of course it's all over now, and we can afford to laugh about it."

"I don't know whether you can afford to laugh about it or not," said Dr. John soberly. "Your position is not so sound as I should like to have it."

"I thought that was all settled long ago," said Ned in surprise. "We have never heard anything since I made the entry" —

"But I have," interrupted the doctor. "I have been following the matter very closely. Your application created quite a tempest in the political teapot at Washington, and it has been raging ever since. The question of your rights has gone from one authority to another. It has traveled from department to department. It has been in the hands of a congressional committee. For a time it looked as if it would be approved; but I will tell you frankly that the latest reports are discouraging."

"On what grounds do they object to granting it?" asked Ned, turning very pale.

"On the ground that you are a minor with a living parent. If your father should regain his health he could of course claim the right which you would have already exercised."

"But he never would!" asserted Martin hotly.

"Our opinion as to that makes no difference in the question of law," said the doctor.

"What are we to do? Give up the land?" asked Ned.

"You have two alternatives open to you."

"And they are?"

"Continue to live on here, as you have been doing, taking your chances of being disturbed by the national authorities or some rival settler, and, if no one interferes before, enter the land again, in proper form, when you are twenty-one. Or — bring your father up here, and amend the entry at once, if the final ruling is adverse, by placing it in his name."

"We can't do that," said Hope, her cheeks burning and her eyes filling. "How can you think, Dr. John, that we would run the risk of sacrificing our father's life for our own selfish benefit?"

"My dear little girl," replied the doctor kindly, "do you suppose I would suggest anything to you that could work any possible injury to your father?"

"Dr. John, do you mean that it would be safe — surely safe — to move our father up here?"

"Perfectly safe, Hope, if you will let my friend manage the moving for you. Your father will not be injured in the least by the journey, if it is made under the proper conditions. I should have advised it from the first, if it had not been for the difficulty of getting here. Now that the bridge is built, that objection is removed. He will be a hundred times better off up here than in any hospital. If I must confess the truth, I don't exactly like the treatment your father is getting professionally. I have disapproved of it all along. They give him too many drugs."

The young people were somewhat puzzled as they listened to this explanation. Evidently the doctor's friend in the city had told him more than he, Dr. John, had thought it best to repeat to them. And how strange to hear a physician denounce the tools of his trade!

The doctor interpreted their thoughts in some degree: —

"Mind, I don't say that we can get him well, or

even promise that there will be any decided improvement. There is n't a man living who can predict the outcome of such a case. I do say that the conditions will be much more favorable; that his chances will be improved. Oh!" exclaimed Dr. John, in a fine rage with the traditions of his school, " when will people learn the sin of shutting patients up in a gruesome city building, surrounded by the sick and the dying, violating the highest demands of nature, and then expecting them to get well? The sanitarium of the future will have pure air, cheerful surroundings, healthful diet, and banishment of drugs for its cornerstone. Of course this is rank heresy for a physician to be preaching. Now, recollect, you young people must n't tell of me, or my profession might ' fire ' me."

"There is another reason why I feel like hastening this change," said Dr. John to Hope as he was leaving the house, after their plans for the sick man's journey had been laid out. "For several months past your father has been making incoherent sounds. I am convinced he is making an effort to control his speech. No one down there understands him or tries to; indeed, no one has the time; but I believe if you and the boys, or any people who cared for him, could be near him all of the time and give him the proper attention, they might come, in time, to make out what he tries to say. It would be a great comfort to him."

CHAPTER XXIX.

HOW GOD REMEMBERED.

ONLY a number in a hospital ward!

How many times Henry Austin had repeated this sentence to himself. He, — all his life a strong and active man earning an independent living and providing a comfortable support for his family, loved and respected, and looked to for counsel and help, — to be for three long years reduced to this!

A number in a hospital ward! checked and billeted and laid by to await that awful day, so terrible when it approaches a man like this, when the sheet would be drawn over his face, and he would be carried off, like other poor fellows he had seen, to lie on a dissecting table or be buried in a pauper's grave.

Three long years! How his soul raged within him, and he strove to break the bonds that held him as he thought upon it. Somewhere he had read of a soldier in the army, sent out on a scouting expedition, and prisoned by the timbers of a fallen building, who found himself looking down the muzzle of his own gun, knowing that the settling of the timbers, at any moment, might sign his death warrant and send a bullet crashing through his brain. The man had finally been rescued, hours later, a raving maniac.

Just so he had lain there and faced death, not minute after minute and hour after hour, but day after day, month after month, year after year. Why had his own brain not given away? How did it come that the delicate mechanism had survived the frenzied beating of the soul against its bars?

A number in a hospital ward, bound hand and foot by disease, unable to give any outward sign of the passionate longings, the bitter regrets, that surged within him. The children he had loved so dearly, left to him as a sacred charge by his dying wife, were struggling on alone, deprived of his help and guidance. Thousands of men who loved their homes and families not half so well as he had loved his, daily passed up and down the street outside, on their way to and from their work. Other men, who had been permitted to retain the brute strength with which nature had endowed them, beat their wives and abused their little children, and spent their days in carousal, while he lay there inert and powerless, an interesting study for medical students, a puzzle for the doctors.

Only a number in a hospital ward! The world going on without him. Forgotten by his old friends. A lost factor in humanity. Forgotten,— yes,—

Forgotten by God!

Others had been remembered.

For three winters the grass had grown over the grave of the man who had been brought there the day he had come, and who had occupied the cot beside him. The poor fellow who had come in last night, his legs crushed by a cable car, was even now being carried out on a plank. He, alone, was forgotten.

The corpse and the men who bore it had gone out, and an oppressive silence reigned in the place.

Perhaps it would be his turn next. Perhaps God would remember.

The door was opening again. There was a short parley. A visitor had arrived. It was no one for him. His visitor, — his heart warmed at the thought, — his one faithful friend raised up for him in a miraculous way, came only on Sunday, and this was Thursday.

Those visits were the one break upon his monotonous existence, the sole thread of connection between him and the life he had left.

What a singular insight this mysterious visitor seemed to have, talking of the things he most liked to hear about, summing up the important news of the week, bringing illustrated papers, which he held so patiently for him to look over, reading aloud something that would give him food for thought during all the dreary week that was to follow. Best of all, he brought news of the children, with little remembrances from them; told of the brave fight they were making, and of their success; assured him that they were growing in mind as well as thriving in a worldly way, and — most precious assurance of all — that their thoughts still clung to him. How greedily he listened to the little homely details of their daily life, the life from which he was barred out, he, whom God had forgotten.

Steps were coming down the ward. He closed his eyes, feigning sleep. He did not want to see the strange faces of other people's friends, did not want to feel the doctor's business grip upon his pulse, or to serve as a text for a disquisition to some new students.

The footsteps were pausing beside his cot, pausing many moments, — minutes. It was not like physicians or students to have so much patience.

He opened his eyes and saw a familiar face, full of compassion, looking down upon him. Had he then lost the count of time, and was the Sabbath come again, bringing with it this kind and never-failing visitor?

"Mr. Austin," said the visitor, "I have come to take you to your children."

Not forgotten! Oh, praise God! not forgotten. To be taken away from the dull ward and stifling city air, out into the country. To see green fields and flowers and fresh green foliage, to hear the birds sing, and the low of cattle, the ripple of running water, the music of his children's voices.

In the excitement of the moment he lifted his

hand, his helpless right hand, which fell again powerless by his side; but the visitor observed the action, and his face brightened.

Doubt, unbelief, a dumb surprise, succeeded by a look of exultation, swept over the face of the invalid. But he glanced fearfully towards the door, where a physician stood talking to the nurse in charge of the ward.

"That's all settled. I have made it all right with them. Now I am going to help to get you ready, and we will start on the noon train."

Under the skilful direction of Dr. John's friend, it took but a short time to make ready the sick man's simple belongings, and to prepare him for the journey, protected by a warm overcoat and fleecy traveling rug, tucked carefully about him, in the great wheeled chair.

As he was carried out of the ward he looked back and saw one of the attendants taking down the card and number from the head of his cot.

A leaden weight seemed to drop from him. His shackles had fallen away.

The great invalid chair was put into the ambulance and carried down to the ferry, with scarcely a jolt or jar of its occupant.

How good the world was, after all, and how kind the people! Willing hands aided in lifting down the invalid, drivers of loaded express teams reined up their horses, hack-drivers turned aside, to give the chair right of way.

Every one looked pitiful, and he heard words of

gentle commiseration on every side. A lady who brushed past him laid a fresh rose in his hand. A little child came and leaned against his chair, looking up into his wasted face with sad, inquiring eyes. Train hands hurried to his companion's side to give him assistance in lifting his charge aboard the train. An old white-haired gentleman (it was Mr. Abbott) followed them into the baggage car, exchanged a few words with his friend, and then turned to the sick man with some warm words of commendation for the children that it did his heart good to hear.

There was quite a little crowd waiting at their destination, Ned and Martin being foremost to welcome him. Every one wanted to help about getting him off the car and into the light spring wagon that was waiting. Many were the cautions given to the driver, many and cordial the expressions of sympathy and interest in him.

He had not only regained his identity once more; he already seemed a person of importance in this small place, and the open solicitude for his comfort, the general anxiety for his safety, moved him to wonder, for the first time during his long illness, whether he might not possibly regain his health after all.

It was so different from being merely a number in a hospital ward.

How carefully the man drove over the smooth road, keeping the horses in a walk all the way, avoiding the little ruts channeled by a recent shower, and the rocks that were now and then exposed, while Dr. John and the boys steadied his chair. How fresh the face of all the country, bathed in the noon sunshine, radiant in its winter verdure.

And now they are drawing near to the hills and crossing a stream of crystal purity, overhung by tall trees. And now they are turning into a little lane bordered by a hedge of roses, and beyond are more roses, brilliant of color and gladdening the air with their perfume. There are still more roses wreathed about the little cottage beyond, and beneath the climbing vines is the daintiest flower of them all, a fair young girl with her hands clasped before her and tears in her shining eyes: his dear little daughter, Hope. Her name should be his watchword henceforth.

As for the children, their joy at seeing their father was quite damped by their failure to see Dr. John's friend.

Martin at length blundered out his surprise and disappointment.

"But your friend, Dr. John? the one who has gone to see father, and sent us news every week, — I thought he was to be here."

Dr. John looked so guilty that Martin was convinced that he had plunged into new depths of crime, and his heart smote him.

CHAPTER XXX.

PROGRESS.

"My friend? Oh, yes. He's a queer sort of chap, Martin. Awkward fellow,— rather keep out of the way. Some other time, perhaps," explained Dr. John, hopelessly confused.

A sudden conviction swelled Hope's heart. She looked into Dr. John's telltale face, and her eyes swam in tears.

"Dr. John, don't we already know your friend? Isn't he right here, before us, now?"

She extended one little hand to the Doctor as she spoke, but he had turned away and did not see it.

"My friend's occupation will be gone now," was all he said in reply.

They had all been busily at work, preparing for their father's coming. The boys had cut a new door into their room and partitioned off half of it for Hope, while in the room she had occupied they put the set of furniture that had always been used by their parents. They had covered the floor with straw matting and had put some coyote skins upon it; there were fresh flowers on the table and bureau, and family photographs upon the wall.

They would have taken the invalid at once to his room, but with a feeble movement of his head, a look of appeal in his dark eyes, he protested so earnestly against going in-doors, that they placed his chair on the porch. There he sat until the sun bowed low in the west, and the chill of a December night came down.

"We must have a Christmas this year, Hope," said Ned, a week or two later, coming in upon Hope as she was giving the last touches to her neat little kitchen, after finishing her morning's work.

"Oh, I mean to," said Hope, with an important, matronly look. "I made mince-meat last week, you know, and that pumpkin out in the garden is for pies."

"I wasn't thinking so much of the eatables, Hope; I knew you could be trusted to look after them and we boys to do justice to them. Let us trim up the house and give it a holiday look, and study up some little surprises for father; make it a sort of celebration of his coming home."

"That will be delightful," cried Hope, her eyes sparkling. "You know how generously he used to provide for us on such days. We must make him understand that it is our turn now."

The young people kept their plans a secret from each other. On the day before Christmas Hope was busy, up to her elbows in flour, beating eggs to a stiff froth, cutting jellies into cubes and spheres and stars, rolling out sheets of flaky paste, watching fire and oven with breathless anxiety.

Mr. Austin's chair had been wheeled into the kitchen that morning, and he watched his young daughter's preparations with a gentle indulgence that soon grew into a subdued interest, and then into an open solicitude, rivaling her own, when the fire flashed up too quickly and threatened to scorch some of the nice things, and dampers had to be pulled out and covers lifted. He tasted the choice tidbits that she brought to him, and answered the anxious inquiry of her eyes with a look of pleased approval. Altogether they had a delightful time of it, father and daughter, conducting these grand preparations together.

Mr. Austin signified his wish to retire early that night. The long, wakeful nights he had spent in the hospital were giving way to sound and wholesome sleep. He was genuinely weary from the passive part he had taken in the bustle and stir of the day, and he fell asleep almost as soon as the boys got him undressed and into his soft, comfortable bed.

He awoke the next morning with a blessed sense that the years had somehow fallen away and his dead wife had come back. In the adjoining room a sweet voice was singing a little Christmas hymn that she used to sing. It took some minutes for him to collect his thoughts and to realize that it was only Hope, singing softly as she went about her work. How like to her dead mother the child was growing every day.

But what had happened to his room? It was

transformed into a veritable bower, with leafy garlands and bunches of mistletoe and flowers. High up on the wall there was an inscription in living green. The letters were clumsily fashioned, but he made them out without much difficulty: —

Merry Christmas.

So that was the meaning of Hope's elaborate preparations the day before! He had not thought it was so late in the year. The days of the week he had always kept account of, but he had grown tired of counting the months.

The boys came in, with suppressed joy in their faces, to get him ready for the day. They washed and dressed him and wheeled his chair up close to the bed, to help him upon it. There came a light tap on the door.

There stood Hope, her face beaming, and on her arm a marvelous dressing-gown made of some soft, heavy cloth, a dark maroon, with silken facings of brightest cherry color, and with tiny sprays of flowers embroidered on the points of the collar and on the cuffs and pocket lapels. I am not prepared to say that it could compare with any tailor-made garment, or that it had much of any shape at all, or that the combination of colors would have stood the test of an artistic critic's scrutiny, but there was so much love and unselfishness and patient industry woven into it, that I should like to see the critic who would have had the heart to find fault with it.

Then came the boys' turn, and Ned brought out a prettily carved reading-rack that he had made, which slipped into a brass socket in the arm of the invalid-chair. Martin had made a pretty tray, just large enough to hold an individual tea-service, and this, too, was arranged so that it could be attached to the chair or taken away at pleasure.

It is wonderful how much can be expressed without the use of ordinary speech. The father's face and eyes spoke volumes of gratitude and content.

It was a disappointment to them all that Dr. John did not come to share Hope's bountiful dinner, but late in the afternoon Wing came over, bringing a huge parcel and a note. The note was addressed to Mr. Austin, and read : —

"I send you with this a Christmas remembrance for Hope. I am sure you will permit her to receive this token from one who has found great comfort in watching her happy, self-denying life, and who once received from her the highest compliment ever paid him."

They removed the paper wrappings from the parcel and found a large pasteboard box. Hope lifted the cover and gave a cry of delight, for there was the realization of her most ambitious dream of self-gratification. A dark brown walking-dress of finest texture and stylish but modest pattern. A pretty hat and walking-jacket and two pairs of gloves to match the dress. Beneath these was another parcel, containing a pair of neat French-kid boots.

The little maid was almost afraid to show the pleasure she felt over these things for fear the others might think she had been unhappy without them, but she soon found that she need have no such scruples. The boys were quite as delighted as she, and would not be satisfied until she had run and put on the pretty clothes and given them all a chance to admire them.

They all wondered at the last clause in Dr. John's letter. None of them recollected Hope's quaint speech when they were riding down to The Brook the first day they came to the ranch: — " You look as if you could be trusted."

The sick man, so long shut up in a shadowed room and between close walls, seemed to have an insatiable desire to be in the open air.

" Let him have it. It is the best tonic in the world," was Dr. John's decree.

So day after day they drew him out upon the porch, or along the paths, grown hard and smooth with three years' constant usage, leading over the place. They humored his whims as a mother studies the fancies of a delicate child. When chill winds arose in the afternoon, and they started to take him back to the house, they yielded to the piteous entreaty of his eyes and fastened up a blanket to break the force of the wind, and muffled him more warmly, feeling richly repaid by his look of gratitude and pleasure.

On rainy days, when he could not be taken out, he was fain to take comfort by the open fire, but his eyes always turned longingly towards the window, and all rejoiced that the stormy days were few and scattering, and the days of warmth and sunshine many.

When summer came, the boys made him a bed of rushes under the old walnut tree in the orchard, where they were accustomed to pack their fruit, and when fall came another couch was made up in the vineyard, with a rude canopy over it.

For the better part of two years he lived, ate and slept out of doors. Before a single year had gone by, what the skill of man had failed to accomplish, nature and God did for him. By degrees the incoherent sounds resolved themselves into words and the words into sentences, too indistinct and broken to be always understood by strangers, but intelligible to those around him.

The mysterious affection which still held the organs of speech in a measure under its spell did not relax its hold upon the muscles of his body. He could not stand upon his feet or hold a sheet of paper in his hand.

In after days the lessons of this sad period came home to the young people. It taught them to value the help and sympathy of others, to appreciate the need of mutual dependence, to cultivate the sweet virtues of patience and unselfishness.

CHAPTER XXXI.

HOW TOM KEPT HIS WORD.

THE second winter that Mr. Austin spent at the ranch was marked by the coldest weather known in California since it came into the possession of the United States.

The mercury, which usually ranged from 45° to 50° Fahrenheit on the most severe winter days, and only on rare occasions touched 32°, began a series of most scandalous performances. First it retreated to a couple of degrees below the freezing point, and the frost played havoc with the leaves of geraniums and a few other tender plants.

At this Californians made merry, for out of their wealth of bloom and fragrance they could for a time well afford to spare the geraniums, — little prized on account of their rank growth and unpleasant odor. The heliotrope they missed more, but knew that a few weeks would restore it. So boys and girls sought eagerly for the thin film of ice that formed on standing water in exposed situations, and men and women congratulated each other upon the crisp, exhilarating air, and accounted for the extreme cold by attributing it to the snow that had lately whitened the summit of the

"Black Hills," as they called the thickly wooded range ten miles back from the valley.

But so far the mercury was only coquetting. It had serious business on hand, and meant to compass it. Just as the people were laughing over the game of hide-and-seek it was playing around the freezing point, and predicting that in twenty-four hours there would come a decided change of weather, the mercury played a shameless joke.

It dropped to 25°, seven degrees below the freezing point.

People who had for a quarter of a century gone to sleep in perfect security against the inroads of the weather awoke to find exposed waterpipes burst and their premises flooded, many delicate vegetables and flowers frozen stiff, growing grain blighted, lime trees killed, and the fruit and foliage of lemon and orange trees withered as if by a hot blast.

Of course they tried to make light of it, and jested, saying that a bit of weather from beyond the Rockies had strayed west and could not find its way back. They deplored the hundreds of lives lost in the middle northwest, up Minnesota and Dakota and Nebraska way, during the terrible blizzards that prevailed there, and congratulated themselves upon their superior position, saying that it had never happened before, that it was nice to have some real "weather" after all, and that it wasn't half as bad as Florida — presumptuous minx! — had done a year or so back; and that it would never happen again; and they were glad of it anyhow, because it gave them a chance to compare their own glorious climate with the East, — and a host of other very comforting and philosophical assertions.

But the fact remained that California was most painfully humiliated. Her "glorious climate" was in tatters. It took months to recover from the shock vegetation received. It took years to recover from the blur upon her reputation.

At Home Ranch, during the prevalence of the "blizzard," as the five days of frosty weather were called, the boys did little for a day or so, except to attend to their stock and the daily chores, seal up cracks around the doors and windows through which the wind whistled, and pile up wood in the great fireplace, where the flames leaped and crackled in defiance of the weather.

Then their boyhood asserted itself, and since the weather tried to make merry with them, they decided to make merry with the weather. So they faced the cool blasts, and took advantage of the crust frozen over the wet ground to draw up great loads of driftwood from the stream. They broke off pieces of ice nearly an inch thick from the sheet that covered the reservoir by the spring, extemporized a freezer, and with their abundant supply of sweet cream made some delectable ice-cream. They even prepared a mimic toboggan slide by flooding a steep declivity near the reservoir, one of the coldest nights, and did some tall and lofty tumbling there with the drag the next day.

The cold period dissolved in a tempest of wind and rain, which will long be memorable on the California coast, because of the good ships it sent to the bottom. Even in San Francisco Bay, vessels dragged their anchors and were tossed helplessly about, so that damaging collisions resulted, while light craft were hopelessly at the mercy of the winds and waves.

On the night that this tempest was brewing, a stylishly dressed young fellow went down to the water-front and ordered a man to get out a sailboat.

The man openly protested.

"It's not a fit night to be out in, sir. There's a moon now, — but look off there."

He pointed to the southwest, where a dark mass of clouds was rising, driving before it a line of fleece white as the ocean's foam.

"Never mind. It doesn't concern you; I'm the one that's going, not you." The man obeyed orders without further protest, but there was a hard, reckless look on the young man's face that he could not forget, and when he had watched the frail boat and its occupant out of sight, he turned in for the night with an uneasy sense that he had neglected his duty.

He awoke later to the roaring of the wind and heard the rain falling in sheets on the roof, and remembered the boat, and the boy who had gone out in it alone.

"Something's up," he said to himself. "Never

saw him like that before; him, always so good-natured and pleasant-spoken. Jiminy! If he's out in this!"

Something was wrong, — miserably, hopelessly wrong.

Father and son, after years of wretched misunderstandings, bad management on the one side and willful defiance on the other, had come to an open issue. Stung by the taunts he had received, the young fellow had started off, bound he cared not whither, but resolved never to return to the man who had disowned him.

Tom Bateman was in the middle of the bay when the squall struck. The moment before he was reckless, desperate, indifferent as to what became of him; but when he saw the caps of foam rising about him and felt the wind strike his small craft, he strove, with the instinct of a true sailor, to help her to weather the gale.

The next moment he saw that it was useless. The wind had chopped around and was coming from the northwest, driving him toward the Alameda shore, against the ebb of a strong tide.

He could only cling to the gunwale and await the inevitable result, a crash against one of the great hulks looming up along the eastern shore, or the capsizal of the boat. In either case he would have little show.

Death was before him, and he was not ready.

Alas for the wasted years that lay behind him! He had always thought there was plenty of time.

Plenty of time to enjoy himself, to have a "good time," to jest and frolic and parley with life, leaving its serious duties for years to come.

And now, the years to come, — where were they?

He was going into an eternity he dared not face, an eternity where he could think of but one who might be pitiful to him and shield him from blame: the little sister who died long years before.

Thinking of the little sister reminded him of the fair young girl who was so like her. It was not a pleasant memory, the recollection of that day when he had come upon her in her country home, and wounded her and shamed himself, in his dastardly attempt to prove himself a man of the world in the eyes of his low companions.

She had not made a failure of life, — neither she nor the boys. His path had been easy and theirs hard, but they had done the best that came in their way, and he, — he had gone straight down to perdition, and this was the end. There was pity in her face that day, in spite of her contempt. Perhaps she would be more pitiful if she could see him now.

Ah! it had come. He was in the water trying to get hold of the capsized boat, which thrust him back and fled from him as if it too were human. It was only a question of a few moments when he should go to the bottom, but he struck out, cumbered as he was by his heavy clothing, clutching, as men will, at the last desperate chance.

He must be close to the other shore. He remembered it, — miles and miles of mud flats, more dangerous far than the open bay. Yet here and there, far apart, were little country wharves, reached by deep estuaries, where grain and other rural products were shipped. If he should happen upon one of these, the chance might become a certainty.

The water was calmer now, for the tide was at the turn, but he had the wind to battle with, now shrieking full in his face, now blowing from all points of the compass at once. But what was this? Deep, clear water, salt no longer, but fresh as a mountain spring, and with dim, ghostly shapes on either side. He clutched at something, exhausted, fainting.

CHAPTER XXXII.

A NEWSPAPER ITEM.

THE next morning dawned clear and bright.

Hope was out early, attending to some little chickens whose coops had been flooded by the rain. She had gathered the wettest of the downy creatures into her apron, and was returning to the house to put them in a basket beside the kitchen stove, when something strange and unearthly seemed to rise up in her path.

She gave a cry of terror, and then stood still and trembling.

A drowned man! There could be no doubt about it. The pallid face, the sunken eyes, the bare, wet head, the dripping clothes! And there was a terribly familiar look about the face. Oh, why should IT come to her?

But drowned people do not walk and speak and smile, — such a ghostly semblance of a smile as it was!

"Don't run away from me, Hope. Don't be afraid. It's a very different way this time — different from the last."

"But, Tom — Tom! What does it mean?" she cried, her voice sharp with a fear that it might not be the living Tom after all, that her very senses might be playing her false.

The man who had tossed about on the water all night, a plaything between life and death, caring little what became of himself, believing that there was no one else to care, was deeply moved by the sight of her distress.

"It means a great deal that I am not able to tell you just now," he said shakily. "It means that old life is all over. It means that if you take me in, you take in an outcast, — one who has his own way to make in the world, and a hard prospect before him. Oh, Hope!" he broke off, "I've been face to face with death all night. It's going to be different after this. Put that other time out of your mind."

"Of course I will," said Hope softly, the tears coming into her eyes, she knew not why.

"But what am I thinking?" she suddenly exclaimed. "You will die if you stand here in your wet clothes. Come into the house. Go into the boys' room and get some of their clothes. Take towels and rub yourself dry before the fire in the front room. Be very quiet. Father is sleeping yet. And — Tom! Be careful what you say before him. We never excite him in any way. We will tell him you have come to pay us a visit, and pass it off that way."

"But the boys?" said Tom.

"Oh, the boys! You know them. It will be all right with the boys."

So it came that Tom Bateman became one of the household at Home Ranch. The boys received him with little question. They were satisfied to know that he had had a disagreement with his father, and had left home for a time. They wondered a little over the episode of the sailboat, but attributed the reckless voyage to a foolish freak rather than any more serious impulse. They did not know but what he was in regular correspondence with his family. It was enough for them that although more sober and thoughtful than they had ever known him, he was the same good-hearted fellow, the same pleasant companion as of old.

With Hope he talked more freely. She alone understood that the scene before father and son, the night he left home, had been the culmination of years of indifference on the father's part, years of undirected license for the son, furthered by the thoughtlessness of a society-loving woman.

"I give you my word, Hope, I had done nothing wrong or shameful. I had only idled away the time and thrown money about, like the other young fellows I knew, — sons of my father's friends, associates of his own pick and choosing. He never encouraged me to do or be anything else. Yet he hauled me over the coals for it. 'You're going to the dogs,' my father said. 'I'm going exactly where you've ticketed me,' I said. Then he flew into a terrible rage, and I would n't stand his abuse and told him so. He ordered me to leave the house and never presume to enter it again, and

I told him I'd take him at his word. My mother stood by and heard it. She never said a word. They did n't care, either of them. They were glad to get rid of me."

"Oh, they did care. They do care," said Hope earnestly when she heard this statement. "They are troubling about you now. You must write to them, or go back."

"I can't do it, Hope. It's gone too far to be mended. If you choose to turn me out here, it's all right" —

"You know that I don't mean that, Tom, but it is n't right to feel so. And it is n't true. Mothers do care, even if they don't show it. And your father, — perhaps you spent too much. Maybe he could n't afford the money, Tom."

"He! He's rolling in money. A million and to spare. Everybody knows it," and Tom laughed bitterly. "Never mind. I'll show him that I'm not dependent on him. I can make my way in the world, even if I have to do it by hoeing peas or following the plow. I'm going to strike Ned for wages next week."

For the first time in his life, Tom Bateman had settled down to steady work. For the first time in his life, his surplus energies were finding a wholesome and legitimate channel, and the discipline was good for him.

The boys looked upon his action as a mere whim, and wondered how soon it would give out, and were quite ready to jest with Tom over his experience in ranching, when the notion should have worn itself out. But when week after week passed by and his term of service extended into months, they began to comprehend that what they had mistaken for a boy's rash impulse was a man's serious purpose.

"It's the only life in the world worth living," he said to Hope one day. "I don't mean that it is absolutely necessary for a man's welfare that he should put forth strong physical effort all his life, though it is a good tonic; but this quiet home life, the reliance upon each other, the interest in growing things, — it somehow binds a family together. If my father had been a farmer it all would have been different."

It was noticeable that he always referred to his family in the past tense, as if they belonged to a life that was finished; but Hope never lost an opportunity to help him to see matters in their true light, as she understood them, and to remind him of his duty. She was frank, even to cruelty, in her arraignment. She censured him unsparingly. She ascribed sentiments to the absent parents that only a tender-hearted girl's fancy could conceive.

At last she won from him a reluctant promise that he would go back.

"But I won't go empty-handed. I am going to take back some money that I have earned by the sweat of my brow," said Tom.

It happened that about this time Mr. Abbott was in need of a book-keeper and time-keeper in his nursery, a happy combination of indoor and outdoor service quite to Tom's taste, and he decided to apply for the place.

He put on the suit of clothes he had worn when he came to the ranch, which had been cleaned and pressed by Hope's skillful hands, and went out to exchange a few words with the boys about some errands he was to do for them in the village, then started down the road.

As he reached the bridge he heard a faint cry, and turned to see Hope following him, with a newspaper in her hand, and a face full of distress.

"Oh, Tom! They did care," she said, extending the paper to him, with a look of compassion.

The paragraph to which she pointed read as follows : —

Matthew Bateman, a well known capitalist, died of apoplexy yesterday afternoon at three o' clock, in his office in —— Block. His death was undoubtedly the direct result of business troubles which have been harassing him for the last year. Although he was a large real-estate owner, he had become entangled in some unfortunate speculations, and it is rumored that he died insolvent.

Mr. Bateman's family consisted of a wife and one son. Several months ago the latter disappeared, but as it was believed he had taken passage upon some ship bound for a foreign port, the matter was not made public. Subsequently, however, it was learned that he went out in a sailboat on the night of the memorable —— of January, and the recent discovery of the remnants of the boat thrown upon the east shore of the bay leaves no doubt as to the young man's untimely fate. This circumstance adds to the melancholy situation of the unfortunate wife and mother, who has never left her bed since the day of her son's disappearance.

"I must take the next train. I must go to the city at once," said Tom huskily.

Then he turned and put his arms around Hope, and drew her to him and kissed her as he might have kissed his own little sister, had she been spared to him.

"Good-by, dear," he said. "Whatever I am — if I ever amount to anything — I owe it all to you."

CHAPTER XXXIII.

THE PRODIGAL SON.

In the great house on California Street in San Francisco, all was changed. Passers-by looked at its neglected garden, its closed blinds and doors, and the heavy folds of crape hanging from the front door-knob, recalling the days when a pompous man of affairs came and went with the regularity of clockwork; when the street before it was alive with carriages waiting upon afternoon receptions and evening parties; when a richly dressed woman passed up and down the steps with gracious dignity, and a merry boy ran in and out.

In a darkened room above, a woman, white as the soft wraps folded about her, was lying on her bed. Her hair, sprinkled with gray, was drawn smoothly back from her sharpened temples, and her thin hands, folded listlessly together, were destitute of ring or ornament.

"It makes my heart ache just to look at her!" sighed a maid, Annette, to her fellow-servitor, James, in the hallway.

"She's a shadder!" said James sententiously.

"And to think of the pretty bloom she always had in her cheeks, and her hair that was a pleasure to 'do up,' it was so soft, and shiny, and wavy; and her silks, and laces, and velvets, and diamonds, and sealskins, all packed away under lock and key. Oh, the trouble that's come on this house!" cried Annette, appealing to the stolid James for sympathy. "The master dead in the room below; master Tom gone, and she a-following them as fast as ever she can. It's enough to wring a body's heart."

"All folks has their thrubbles, but it do seem the Lord is after sinding more than its share an this house," remarked James dryly.

A feeble voice was faintly calling Annette's name. She hastened to obey the summons, and found Mrs. Bateman propped up on one arm, a feverish flush in her cheeks, and her eyes bright with anxious expectation. She was trying to look through a doorway leading into the adjoining room.

"Is everything ready, Annette? Is the table set in there as usual? You know he may come to-night."

"Everything, Mrs. Bateman."

"You remembered the anchovies and the sandwiches, and the cup of hot coffee over the gas?"

"Yes, madame. Please lie down. Everything will be all right if he comes."

Tears were trickling down the girl's cheeks as she gently forced the invalid down, re-arranging her pillows with a pat and stroke. In the hall outside she burst out crying, sobbing so violently, albeit under breath, that the sight of her sorrow affected even the callous James.

"Oh, come, Miss Annette. It can't help matters, carrying on so. What's up, anyhow?"

"It's only the same old thing, James. The table all set out for master Tom in her little parlor, where she used to leave a nice supper fixed up for him when he stayed out late and missed his dinner. Never the least difference, though I was by and heard when the lawyer and Mr. Bateman broke it to her last week, about the boat being cast ashore and him at the bottom of the bay. I misdoubt me she's losing her mind, through all this misery."

"Annette," said James slowly and with deliberation, "sure you'll be knowin' the owld proverb about the bad shillin'?"

"The 'bad shilling'!" echoed Annette, wiping her eyes with her apron, and staring at him in her perplexity. "And what has the bad shilling to do with my mistress and her dead?"

"It's me, Annette, that knows the young master an' his thricks the bist av all," continued James sagely. "It's me that's attinded an him an' been throdden under fut by him, as ye might say, fer more years than ye've told, me girl. Wasn't it him that throwed his t'y locomotive at me head, — in a fine passion he was, though still in skirts, — an' give me this scar here be the same token?"

James pointed with something like pride to the indistinct white line marking an old cut on his forehead.

"An whin he got oulder," he continued, "what wid his bull-pups an' game fowls an' evadin' the law concernin' thim; an' his white rats an' parrots an' machinery an' trash an' divilment widout end — oh, it's a rare dance he's led me all alang. Shud I live to the age av Methuselah I'll niver fergit the mornin' I found the gopher snakes kiled up in me boots, to thry me whether I'd been takin' a drap too much on goin' to bed the night afore. An' the illictric shock he give me alang av his new batthery only last winter wud have killed a horrse, — thim wuz the docthor's own wurruds whin the rascal got him to bring me to agin."

"I did n't think you'd lay up such things, James, and be counting them at this time," said Annette reproachfully. "And he always so free-handed and kind-hearted; so ready and anxious to make it up when he did anybody a harm."

"All the silver he iver flung at me cud n't put from me mind the slimy touch av thim snakes, ner restore me standin' in the eyes av the widdy Mc-Kinstry, — her that has the foine account down at the Hibernia, — since he jerked off me wig wid a fishhook the day I wuz settin' beside her in her cozy garden," replied James with severity. "No, no, it's me that knows the b'y better than none other. But as for countin' his sins, my dear, there's not a day ner hour but what I go over thim, an' wid as good a heart as if I'd be a-tellin' the virtues av the saints."

"I'd like to know what your queer talk means," said Annette.

"It manes that there's somethin' onnatural an' onrale in the dyin' out av masther Tom an' his divilment. It manes that I'm av the same mind wid the misthriss. It wud n't surprise me any moment shud masther Tom come walkin' in an' hit me an the back, till me breath wuz knocked out av me. Ye know the sayin' as to the kind av payple that 'll niver be drowned?"

"Out upon you and your sayings!" cried little Annette, forgetful for the moment of the time and hour. "Oh, you wicked, hard-hearted man! If ever a ghost came back to haunt any one, master Tom's ghost ought to come after you this minute."

"There's some one openin' the front door," said James. "I'd betther be seein' who it may be."

He started down the stairs, but as he reached the first landing he gave a startled exclamation, echoed by Annette a moment later. For slowly mounting the steps there came Tom Bateman; silent and grave, stepping lightly and carefully, the old joyous bound forgotten, the light-hearted, boyish look forever gone from his face. Passing them by, unheeding, he went straight to the quiet chamber where his mother was lying.

"Mother! Poor little mother!"

"Oh, Tom!"

There was never any need of explanation between these two. From this sacred hour in which they mingled their tears over the dead father and husband lying below, — the man so little understood by the one, so thoughtlessly neglected by the other, — trivial misunderstandings were swept away. In the new light that had come upon him the son recalled unnumbered deeds of tender remembrance and forethought received at the hands of both parents in bygone days.

"But, Tom, you have come into a heritage of care," said the mother at length. "The estate is badly involved. Your father died a poor man. We have nothing, nothing at all. This bed I lie upon may be taken away to-morrow. For me it does not matter; it is not probable that I shall live long; but you, poor boy!"

"Mother, you shall get well!" said the young man, some of his old spirit returning. "As for me, since I went away I have found a richer inheritance than father could have left me, if his bank account had been increased a hundred-fold."

"Found an inheritance! A rich inheritance? I don't understand, Tom."

He held out his hands, browned and calloused with labor. He bared his right arm, where the muscle stood out like a cable. He stood up, tall and strong and resolute before her.

"I have found out myself," he said.

CHAPTER XXXIV.

HOPE'S EXPERIMENT.

In the early days of her rose-growing, Hope had tried a little experiment in rose culture.

One day she plucked two wild roses, and carrying them to the darkest of her red roses in the rose garden, held each of them over an open blossom and tapped them gently, stirring the stamens with a blade of wild grass, so that the pollen fell in a fine golden shower. Then she dusted the same roses, a second time, with pollen from the pink climbing roses by the house, and when she had finished she marked the roses on the bush with bits of thread of different colors.

Three months later, when the vessels of the latter were a glowing vermilion, she gathered them and planted their contents in a corner of the boys' cold frame.

At last, to her joy, first one tiny red leaf and then another pushed their way through the ground, and in a short time a row of trim little plants rewarded her patience.

It seemed as if these plants would never bloom. Again and again Hope searched them over to find the promise of a bud, but for a long time in vain.

"You lazy vagrants!" she exclaimed, one morning. "You worthless, indolent paupers! I've the greatest mind in the world to dig you up, root and branch, and burn you."

"What's that, my girl?" cried a pleasant voice, and Hope looked up to find Dr. John watching her.

"Some lazy roses, Dr. John," she answered, a little shamefacedly. "See how large and hearty they are, — yet never a bud have they shown yet, and I'm particularly interested in them, doctor. I wouldn't care so much if they'd do something; no, not if they bore roses as black as a coal!"

After this Dr. John kept an eye to that especial row of roses, however. At length Hope's wish was gratified, but one plant after another developed common pink roses, identical with the pink climber beside the house.

There was one of the seedlings, the largest and most vigorous of all, which obstinately refused to blossom. Over this plant, unknown to each other, Hope and the doctor kept a vigilant watch.

Winter passed, and spring arrived. Early in March a small green bud appeared on this bush, which grew larger and larger, day by day. It was really a very absurd little bud, and so were the multitude of others which soon appeared to keep it company. They were fat and clumsy, and wrapped in homely coats of the darkest green, which kept jealous guard over their contents, letting not the tiniest rift disclose the close-folded petals within.

During the fifth spring they spent at Home Ranch, it happened that early one March morning, while the hills still cast their grateful shadow over the place, Hope, running down from the house to wage war upon some voracious slugs before washing the breakfast dishes, met the doctor coming up from below. Both of them stopped, amazed, and viewed the rosebush with awed and wondering eyes.

For lo! A miracle had been wrought in the night, and poised upon the topmost branch was a superb and beauteous bloom.

Hope's scornful challenge to the bush to produce a "black rose" had been answered in a startling manner, for there before her was certainly the blackest rose ever seen. It was large and globular in form, and each curved petal about the outer margin was edged with vivid carmine, deepening to ruby and deepest maroon, while the heart of the flower was a velvety black, which seemed nevertheless aglow with deep flame tints.

All the air around seemed to pulsate with its rich perfume.

"Oh, I never imagined anything could be so beautiful!" exclaimed Hope, with one deep-drawn breath.

"It is matchless!" declared the doctor, scarcely less excited than she. "But where did you get it, Hope? Out with your secret!"

"I bred it myself," answered the young girl proudly. "I did n't tell anybody what I was doing for fear they 'd laugh at me, and all the others turned out so commonplace," explained Hope.

"Laugh at you!" repeated Dr. John with feeling. "My little girl, I believed you have achieved a very rare distinction: one of which many foreign personages of rank would feel proud, and which would be regarded as a very important exploit by people who make a business of breeding flowers. But what are you doing? Why, Hope, how could you?"

For the young girl had raised her scissors, and with one quick movement the severed flower lay in her outstretched hand.

"Father must see it while it is fresh. You know the ground is wet and he cannot very well come to it. There are plenty of buds left on the bush."

This little act of daughterly devotion touched the doctor. That was always the way at Home Ranch. The best of everything was carried to father, just as all the little worries and discouragements were scrupulously kept from him.

The invalid was at his accustomed post, in the great easy-chair out in front, where it was always wheeled on fair days, when he did not go to orchard or vineyard. His eyes brightened with pleasure as Hope laid the beautiful rose in his right hand, after first lifting it to his face that he might inhale the perfume.

Dr. John told him the story of Hope's experiment, and Mr. Austin smiled proudly on his young daughter.

"You must name it, little woman," said the

doctor. "Here is a chance to make your name immortal. Think of sending your name down through the ages as the sponsor of such a flower!"

To his surprise Hope shook her head, then bowed it until it rested on her father's shoulder, while one arm passed around his neck.

"If I might — I would like to give it — my mother's name," she replied softly.

Mr. Austin's eye moistened. He spoke for the first time in many days in Dr. John's presence, and although his voice was husky, his utterance was clearer than they had known it to be since his attack.

"The — Agnes — Clifford," he said brokenly.

So the rose was christened, and the little family rejoiced in its loveliness, while the doctor joined them, little guessing the important part it was to play in the working out of his own destiny.

CHAPTER XXXV.

HOPE'S BLACK ROSE AND WHAT CAME OF IT.

"Hope," said Dr. John one day in July, "have you ever done anything about that wonderful black rose of yours, the Agnes Clifford?"

"I took a hundred slips from it in the spring, and the most of them are nicely rooted. This fall I shall take some more. I thought — its being so different from any that other people have here — there might be a sale for plants, and I should like to make something directly out of the roses, to make up for — that time, you know. I have n't let it bloom much, but it is the hardest thing to stop it. I never saw such a persistent bloomer. It does seem as if I am pinching off buds all the time."

"A very valuable quality," remarked Dr. John seriously. "All the dark red roses I can find any record of are among the hybrid perpetuals, blooming at the most but twice a year. Even a bright red is a rare color among the ever-bloomers. If this blooms as late as it does early, it will certainly take a front rank among roses when it becomes known. But to have it properly introduced, you ought to put it in the hands of some leading florist."

"I might send it to the florists I ordered the most flowers from. I think they are the leading rose-growers. But I should n't know how to go about it," confessed Hope, frankly.

"Let me manage the correspondence for you," proposed the doctor, taking out his note-book and pencil. "I'll write to them to-night. Now give me the name and address of the firm."

"It is n't a firm. It is just one man," returned Hope. "It is Robert L. Marshall of Philadelphia."

"*Robert L. Marshall!*"

Dr. John's face blanched. Martin, who was near, saw his hand shake. The doctor made no pretense of writing down the address.

"Robert L. Marshall. And of Philadelphia? are you sure?" he asked of Hope, and to Martin there was a note of shrinking cowardice in the voice that made the boy recoil.

What was there in Dr. John's past that dragged its black shadow over his life, and made him terrified at the mere sound of a name? Oh, if the doctor would only have the courage — the manliness — to face it! Martin watched him with a sickening sense of shame at his weakness and fear.

"Robert L. Marshall, I am sure," replied Hope. "But I can write myself, Dr. John," she added quickly. "It is selfish for me to tax you when you have so much to do."

Hope, too, had noticed the doctor's agitation, but innocently ascribed it to a simple cause. She thought he was tired and nervous.

"Oh no, I will write, as I proposed," replied Dr. John, who was himself again. "But it had better go in your name. I will make a rude draught of what I think ought to be said, and you can copy it out in your own hand."

The next day Dr. John handed Hope the promised letter, repeating, in a very emphatic way, his desire that she should copy it out in her own hand.

She sat down at once and made a copy of the letter; but when she had finished her copy she compared it with Dr. John's, and smiled at the contrast. He had called his a "rough draught," yet how finished and scholarly it looked beside her own. What a beautiful, distinctive hand Dr. John wrote, so different from any other she had ever seen! What peculiar twists and turns he gave to certain letters, yet how symmetrical the page looked!

With a willful little nod of her head, she folded up Dr. John's letter, enclosed it in an envelope, sealed and directed it, and gave it to Martin to mail.

Days of anxiety, alternated with pleased anticipation, passed by. One, two, three, four, five, six! The letter must have reached its destination. Then she counted the days again: one, two, three, four, five, six, seven! On the thirteenth day after the letter was dispatched, she appealed to Dr. John.

"Oh, Dr. John, *do* you think he will trust the description, or will I have to send a rose or plant to him?" she cried. "And if he should make it one of the novelties of the season, and let me supply the orders, wouldn't it be grand? But, doctor! Who are those gentlemen coming up the path? See! the taller one looks like a soldier, but he walks with a cane and limps. I never saw them before."

But Dr. John, after one hasty look at the newcomers, vanished without a word, betaking himself in the direction of the house, and Hope was left alone, to face them.

They were coming along the garden path that the doctor had so often trod, looking at the roses on either side as they advanced. As they reached the place where the young girl stood, and beheld the bush beside which she loitered, still proudly upholding its wealth of bloom, the elder gentleman stopped, electrified by the sight, while the younger looked with even more interest at the pure-faced girl.

"Is this the rose?" asked the elder man.

"Sir, you are" — began the blushing girl with dignity.

"Robert L. Marshall, of Philadelphia. And this is my young nephew, Lieutenant Hobart Marshall, fresh from West Point. You see I am here to answer your letter in person. You are Miss Hope Austin, I suppose?" and he touched his hat, with a stiff, military salute.

"Yes, sir," said Hope, simply.

"I happen to be one of the veterans who are

gathering here this month," explained Mr. Marshall, "so we must hold the Grand Army responsible for my promptness; though I am not sure but the rose would justify three thousand miles of travel. It is magnificent."

He did not tell the girl that he had quite made up his mind to forego the Grand Army Reunion that year, but had packed up his luggage within a couple of hours from the time her letter had arrived, and traveled night and day to reach the Western Coast.

He merely drew one of the roses toward him, and studied it with the eye of a connoisseur.

"And is it really new?" asked the trembling girl.

"It is entirely new, to the best of my judgment," replied the veteran.

"I am so glad," said Hope, with a happy smile. "Will you walk up to the house, Mr. Marshall? My father is an invalid, but he will be glad to see you."

They passed on up to the house, where, strangely enough, there was no sign of the doctor. Mr. Austin sat outside, in his easy-chair, and Martin and Ned were both there, resting in the cool shade of the pepper-trees.

The visitors took in the situation with ready tact, and the elder talked with Hope and her father, accepting the invalid's stammering monosyllables and weak gestures of assent with as grave and unquestioning comprehension as if they had been the most finished speeches. The lieutenant entertained Ned and Martin with amusing anecdotes of his academical experiences, or drew from the boys information regarding their own life and work. During a little lull in the conversation they overheard the elder gentleman say to Hope : —

"Miss Austin, you write a very clear and beautiful hand for a young lady. Permit me to congratulate you on it."

Was it only Martin's fancy, or was the veteran eying Hope keenly from beneath his shaggy eyebrows?

"I am sorry — I must confess — I did n't write it myself," replied the girl, flushing.

"Ah! One of your brothers, I suppose, conducts the business correspondence of the ranch?"

"No, sir. Our friend Dr. John drew up the letter, to give me an idea of what I ought to write. I liked the looks of his letter so much better than my own that I sent it."

The lieutenant gave a light, boyish laugh of approval at this frank confession. His uncle rebuked his levity with a glance.

"Dr. John! A peculiar name. What sort of a man is Dr. John, my dear, and where does he live?"

"Just across The Brook," answered Hope. "As to what sort of man he is, I don't think any one person could tell you. You should ask the whole district. He is just the kindest and most thoughtful and generous" —

The visitor cut her short with another keen glance from under his shaggy eyebrows.

"What type of man is he physically? Is he tall or short, light or dark?"

"You must see him for yourself. He is like other men, and unlike them," answered Hope.

"How long has he lived here?"

"Oh, I don't know, sir. Ever so long."

"How far does this famous doctor's practice extend?"

"He has calls from all over the country," said Ned, proudly. "All up and down the valley, and from the bay to ten miles back into the mountains. He's been here so many years, you know; and people think they can't get well without him."

"Ever go down as far as Oakland?"

"Not as a rule, sir."

"Ah! And I suppose he makes all his purchases at one of the villages around here. Gets his horse shod here, patronizes a country butcher, a country tailor, grocer, druggist, — deposits his money in some grangers' bank, eh?"

There was something so peculiar and sinister in this question, following as it did upon the others, that, Ned looked keenly at the gentleman, as if challenging his right to make such inquiries regarding the doctor.

Martin flung himself into the breach.

"Yes, sir," he stoutly replied. "Dr. John puts all his money in the B—— bank," naming a little village several miles away. "Goes there regularly every month. Says he wouldn't trust another bank in the State."

It was the first deliberate falsehood that had ever passed the boy's lips.

The visitors arose to go.

"I must see you again about your rose, Miss Hope," said the older man, kindly. "I shall be in this vicinity for some time."

Martin heaved a sigh of relief as the two figures crossed the bridge. If that were only the last of them! But no! The tall gentleman with the hawk-like eyes had said that they would remain in the neighborhood.

What their motive was the boy could not guess, but well he knew that it boded no good to Dr. John.

CHAPTER XXXVI.

MARTIN TRIES TO SAVE DR. JOHN.

MARTIN was not the only one who speculated over the strange motives that brought Colonel Marshall (for they soon learned that was his title, honorably won in the war of the Rebellion), to the little country inn, together with his handsome nephew.

At the village the colonel and his nephew posed as enthusiastic anglers. When they were not on the porch of the little hotel or loitering around the post-office, they were sure to be somewhere up The Brook, equipped with rod and line and fishing baskets which they oftenest brought back empty. They frequently called at Home Ranch, and often made errands there for fruit and milk, to eke out their noon-day luncheon.

Meanwhile the few who knew him best could not fail to note Dr. John's strange behavior.

Instead of setting out upon his routine of professional visits with the regularity of clockwork, after his usual custom, he seemed to vary his hours every day, and sometimes started out in early morning, sometimes at noon, and sometimes not until late in the afternoon; he invariably drove along the highway at mad speed, while he shrank back into his buggy, looking to neither right nor left.

Martin alone understood. The doctor was in hiding. Had he not seen a face at Dr. John's upper windows, stealthily watching the two anglers as they lounged up-stream? Had he not seen Dr. John hurry out to the stable and drive off on a mad race over the country, as soon the two men disappeared from sight? Why did the doctor come over to see them only when the colonel and his nephew had gone to the city? And why did he ask him — Martin — to bring his mail from the post-office? Why did the hunted look on the doctor's face deepen day after day, until he reminded the imaginative boy of some wild animal brought to bay?

A scrap of conversation which the boy overheard one day served to confirm his worst suspicions. He had followed Colonel Marshall and Lieutenant Hobart up-stream to give them a basket of luscious apricots, which they had engaged on their way. He heard their voices floating out of a leafy covert that overhung a deep pool, famous for trout.

The first word that he caught was the doctor's name. Martin was a young fellow who would have scorned the very suggestion of eavesdropping, but there is such a thing as over-riding one's dearest principles for the sake of a friend.

He stood still and listened.

"Two weeks' time already gone, and not so much

as a square look at this Dr. John yet!" The colonel spoke impatiently.

"Yet you felt sure he was the man, that day we met him on the road,— fast as he drove, and with his hat pulled down over his face," said the lieutenant.

"Sure? Of course I'm sure," insisted the colonel testily. "I tell you I should recognize that handwriting if I came across it on a papyrus in an Egyptian tomb. It's unmistakable."

"Then why don't you go straight to his house, uncle, and corner him there?"

"There you have me, Hobart," confessed the colonel. "There is an element of uncertainty. What could I do, what could I say, if it should not be the right man after all?"

"I don't see anything for it, Uncle Robert, but for you to come down with an attack of the gout, and send for him; though how you could be justified in contracting it on such fare as we have at that snuffy old tavern"—

"And there is the danger that at any moment he may take fright and make off to Mexico or Japan or South America, putting me to endless expense and trouble," pursued the colonel, seriously. "For now that I'm on his track at last, I'll never give up until I've got him."

But here Martin, who had heard quite enough, made his appearance, and the conversation changed.

Was it any wonder that Martin looked forward with apprehension to the time that was coming for that dreaded semi-yearly drive to Oakland? He had become quite hardened to it by this time, and looked upon his part in the errand as a disagreeable duty he was glad to discharge, but he felt unaccountably disturbed as he thought of starting out under the colonel's sharp inspection.

Yet he had not the heart to show any reluctance when the doctor one day hailed him, and said: —

"Well, Martin, ready for a long ride to-morrow?"

"Why, certainly. Of course, Dr. John," stammered the young fellow.

"I want to make an early start, — six o'clock at the latest. Will you be on hand?"

"Yes, sir," replied Martin, secretly hoping that he might wake up sick the next morning, that Dr. John might have an urgent call from some patient in another county, that his horse might cast a shoe, — anything to prevent the engagement from being kept.

But none of these fatalities occurred. They started at the appointed time and sped away over the smooth road leading city-ward.

As they reached the outskirts of the town, Martin, hitherto torn by conflicting anxieties and doubts, came to a new resolution.

He would warn the doctor. The time for reserve, for all false delicacy, had gone by. The doctor must be brought to a realizing sense of his position and the danger in which he stood. It would be a sin to keep silence any longer.

But how difficult it is for a person with any

delicacy or sentiment to talk plainly to a friend, and on such a subject! Six separate times the boy nerved himself to his task, and six separate times subsided into silence, with the fateful words trembling on his lips. He moved so uneasily upon his seat, and turned suddenly upon the Doctor so many times, only to turn away as suddenly, that Dr. John, observing his pale face and agitation, was stirred to a professional interest.

" What's the matter, Martin? Cramps? Been eating too many green apples? "

Now it is not a pleasant thing to have your solicitude for a friend's spiritual welfare construed into an attack of indigestion, by the object of your anxiety, and Martin was half inclined to abandon Dr. John to his fate. But he remembered all that they owed the doctor, and pondered the colonel's savage threat, and nerved himself for one more effort.

" Oh, I'm well enough. You — you need n't mind me, Dr. John. But I wanted to speak to you about a matter of the greatest importance. And please don't drive so fast, Dr. John, and don't be offended with me for speaking about it. It's been such a long time, you know " —

Martin had fairly launched out at last, and there is no doubt that his momentum would have carried him to the point at which he was aiming, but an unexpected interruption occurred at that moment.

A stout farmer, who was returning from town, on espying Dr. John reined up his horses, and began to ask his advice about his wife, who had been ailing seriously for weeks past. This appeal to the doctor's professional knowledge banished the careworn look he had worn, and quickened his generous instinct of helpfulness. When the farmer had driven on again Dr. John turned pleasantly to Martin.

"You were saying something, Martin. Of course you can speak to me freely. Don't be afraid of offending me."

Martin gave one searching look at the kind and honest face turned upon him, and his courage fled. How could he tell a man who looked like that, that he knew him for a detected criminal, that spies were even now upon his track, that prison gates yawned before him!

"Well, Martin, what is wrong?" urged the doctor.

"Oh, it's only — nothing but Beauty. She's got a sort of boil on her neck. We don't know whether to open it or poultice it"—

The absurdity of such an appeal, following such a prelude, struck Dr. John so forcibly that he laughed outright.

"Poultice it by all means, if Beauty will submit to it. I assure you, Martin, that 'never use the knife where flaxseed will do the business,' is one of the most solemn tenets of the medical profession."

Martin was red with wrath at himself, at Dr. John, and at the circumstances that had conspired to move him to make a goose of himself.

CHAPTER XXXVII.

DR. JOHN IS BROUGHT TO BAY.

Martin's wrath subsided and Dr. John grew serious as he reined his horse in a new place, a couple of blocks back of the business centre.

"Here, Martin," he said, handing the boy a stout leather purse. "Go to the Oakland Savings Bank this time. Have it made out to the same person: do you remember? and give in any name you choose; better a woman's. Don't wait a moment after you are through."

Everything favored Martin; it was half an hour after the time of opening and there were few people there. The money was paid in, and counted, and handed over for deposit in the vault. The draft was made out and about to be placed in Martin's hands, when an electric bell sounded.

"Just excuse me a moment," said the clerk who was waiting upon Martin, and he stepped into an inner office.

The boy's keen ears caught the sound of low voices in consultation there. He was half disposed to slip out of the building unperceived, but his feet seemed frozen to the spot. His mind was a blank. He wished with all his heart Dr. John had instructed him as to what he should do in case of serious trouble, for he felt as incapable of intelligent reasoning or action as a babe.

There was a stir in the glass office. The clerk reappeared, accompanied by the president of the bank and — oh, horror! Colonel Marshall.

Colonel Marshall coolly possessed himself of the draft, and fixed his hawk-like eyes upon Martin.

"Now, young man," he said, "make a clean breast of it and save us further trouble. What person gave you this money?"

"Nancy Brown," replied Martin promptly, loyal to his trust, although he shook from head to foot.

"'*Nancy Brown*'!" repeated the colonel, satirically. "This reads '*Susan* Brown.'"

"I mean — I meant to say Susan," insisted the wretched Martin. "They — she sometimes calls herself 'Nancy,' you know."

"Oh, *she* does, does *she?*" commented the colonel with a very uncomfortable emphasis on the pronoun.

"Now, Martin," he urged, speaking kindly and persuasively, "own up that Dr. John sent you, or look me in the eye and tell me that he did not."

"I can't tell you that he did, when he did not, can I?" persisted the lad, trying hard to meet the keen eyes and ignobly failing.

There was a brief silence. Martin felt that shame hung out her flaming banners in his cheek, but he pursued his momentary advantage.

"If you will please to give me that paper, sir! Mrs. Brown is waiting for it and she is in a hurry."

With a quick movement he caught up the paper, as the colonel's fingers unwillingly relinquished their hold upon it. He walked with dignity to the door, the way seeming interminably long. Once outside, he dashed down the steps and ran swiftly up the street, feeling, rather than hearing, pursuers at his back.

He turned into the Twelfth St. market and raced through it without slackening his speed, to the astonishment of fish, vegetable, and fruit venders. He turned down lanes and alleys, doubling upon his own path, ran to the right, to the left, and to the right again, and finally slipped down an alley and out again upon the street opposite the place where he had left the doctor, triumphant in having eluded pursuit, the paper in his hand, joy in his eye.

Just as he came in sight of the buggy, Colonel Marshall and his nephew, approaching from opposite directions, closed in upon it.

"Oh, Martin!" exclaimed Dr. John with one reproachful look at the youth.

"Run to cover at last, old fellow!" cried the colonel, in a resonant voice.

The doctor's face would have moved a stone to pity. Pale and silent, he stared at the colonel as if there arose before him some terrible phantom of the buried past.

"Yes, I knew, Marshall, knew you were here;

knew this was coming. It is useless to strive against destiny."

"You knew! And you have the face to tell me so?" sternly demanded the colonel. "Eighteen years I've been looking for you"—

Lieutenant Hobart gave Martin's arm a violent jerk. "Come along. You ride back with me. My uncle will take care of your 'Dr. John,'" he said.

Martin resisted.

"I'm going to stay here," he said doggedly, freeing himself from young Marshall's grasp.

To his surprise, Dr. John seconded the lieutenant.

"Go along with him, Martin," he said decisively.

Martin had no choice but to obey. He loitered long enough, however, to see the colonel get into Dr. John's buggy and drive off in another direction. He could see that the two men were in earnest conversation, the colonel insisting upon something, the doctor resisting.

Whatever Dr. John's humiliation, Martin felt a miserable comfort in the reflection that he was at least bearing his own share. He could not reply to the lieutenant's gay sallies on the way home. Young Marshall seemed in particularly happy spirits, and sang, and jested, and merrily commented on passing sights with a levity that disgusted Martin as much as it exasperated him.

At last he turned savagely upon the young man: "How can you be so jolly, when you've been a witness to such a scene as that : seen your uncle drag a good man — yes, sir, a good man ! — in the dust. I don't care what you say ; I don't care what the doctor's been or done when he was young ; he's a good man to-day. Ask any one in the valley. Ask the sick people he's made well. Ask the dying he's brought back to life. Ask the poor, — yes, and the bad ones, and they'll all tell you there isn't one who's been so much to them. And yet you, you and your uncle, come here to dig up some old skeleton and disgrace him."

The lieutenant gave vent to a prolonged whistle, expressive of amazement, amusement, and a dozen other sentiments.

"Martin," he said, very irrelevantly, as Martin thought, " suppose you go over to the city with me to-night. The veterans of General —— Post No. 1 are going to have a camp-fire, and a jolly good time they always make of it. You've never seen anything of the kind, and it will liven you up."

Martin was completely nonplussed at this singular invitation, coming under such peculiar circumstances. In his surprise and embarrassment he did what many older people have done in like quandaries. He went directly counter to his own inclinations, and agreed to go.

CHAPTER XXXVIII.

AT THE CAMP FIRE.

Martin did not see the colonel when he and the lieutenant took the down train that night. He had a dim consciousness that not far away, on the platform and in the gathering gloom, stood two muffled figures, and that there was something strangely familiar about them. But he asked Lieutenant Hobart no questions, and, oddly enough, the light-hearted, talkative young fellow was for once silent and preoccupied.

Martin himself was in no mood for merry-making. Only that day he had seen his best friend crushed and humiliated, and borne away like a convicted felon. He had told those at home something of what he had been through, and had been glad to escape from the gloom that had settled over the little household.

He did not feel at all like seeking amusement for himself. A terrible picture was before his eyes, of an ill-lighted, grated cell, wherein sat a man, his face buried in his hands, given over at last to overwhelming despair. Whenever this figure raised its face, the reproachful eyes seemed to seek his own, and he heard again the doctor's sharp exclamation: "Oh, Martin!"

If he could only find out where they had put the doctor, and see him for just five minutes. Then he could explain to him how hard he had tried to save him. A vague idea possessed him that by keeping close to the lieutenant he might contrive to get the ear of Colonel Marshall, and somehow influence him in regard to Dr. John.

They crossed the ferry, and took seats in the cable car, which bore them to their destination. Still absorbed in his own thoughts, young Marshall led the boy up a broad stairway, to where a couple of sentinels guarded the entrance to the room occupied by the Post.

A heavy door swung open and noiselessly closed behind them. They found themselves in a large hall, lighted only by the glow from a great fireplace, where a pile of mimic logs, cunningly surrounded by gas jets, cast a ruddy light on the grizzled veterans, some seated and some standing in the foreground, deepening the shadows in the background.

What a buzz of voices, fusillade of fun and battery of jest! The old soldiers chattered and gossiped like a parcel of girls let loose from school. Sometimes the conversation was confined to little knots and groups; sometimes it was general, as some absorbing topic of common interest was introduced, and several of the brightest speakers took the floor. Occasionally it was interrupted by the entrance of old comrades; now and then it ceased altogether, as all hearkened to the narration of some thrilling incident of battle, or paid the tribute of silence to the mention of the gallant dead.

At length, from the darkened shadows of the outer circle, a tall and commanding figure arose. The firelight fell full on his face, and before he commenced to speak, Martin recognized Colonel Marshall. In spite of the young fellow's prejudice he could not help a thrill of admiration at the veteran's soldierly bearing, his intelligent, aristocratic old face, the resounding voice that penetrated the hall, commanding instant attention.

"Comrades, the veterans of the Rebellion are answering a new roll call. Their ranks on earth are thinning faster than ever before shot and shell. Each year that we come together we miss familiar faces. Advancing years only serve to strengthen the ties that bind us together, and the memory of those who fought and bled and fell beside us in the conflict of twenty odd years gone by.

"Many of us are united by ties antedating the commencement of the great struggle. The company in which I enlisted, at the breaking out of the war, was largely recruited from the students of a college in the town where I was born. Some of us were already nearing thirty; many had just attained their majority. Even in the preparatory department, half-grown lads, fired with patriotic zeal, came forward to enlist, and then returned to school, crestfallen at being disqualified by lack of years.

THE ABANDONED CLAIM.

"You all remember Jack Sherwood, the major of our regiment. A few who are here to-night will recall him as one of those disappointed, humiliated boys. But Jack was not to be daunted in his resolve to fight for the preservation of our Union. He forsook school, plunged heart and soul into the study of medicine, and in less than a year came down to the battle front as assistant surgeon.

"You know how he worked in the field, as cool and brave as any soldier in the corps, giving food and drink to the wounded, and carrying them to places of safety, with bullets whizzing about him. You remember how he stepped into the ranks the day he was eighteen, and rose by degrees to lieutenant, captain, and major. But you don't know that he might have been your colonel, and I remained where I was beneath him, if he had n't told a lot of stuff about me, that day we made our last desperate charge at Chattanooga, and insisted on my being promoted over his head.

"Some of you know what happened afterwards: how he came out of the army in feeble health, and tried to take up the practice of his profession when neither mind nor body was able to sustain the effort. It was like Major Sherwood, when he found himself a broken-down man, when he saw no future before him except as a physical wreck, an incumbrance, as he thought, to family and friends, to steal away from those who would have found their best happiness in caring for him, to go off among strangers to suffer in silence. . . . There were some of us who couldn't give him up. There is not a State in the Union, scarcely a town of any size, where some of us, at one time or another, have not made inquiries for him. When California was designated as the meeting-place of the Grand Army this year, advancing age and business cares weighed so heavily upon me that I at first thought I could not come. One day a letter that I received caused me to change my mind."

The colonel's speech had all along been delivered in a peculiarly jerky and abrupt fashion. As he neared the close he seemed to have difficulty in framing what he wished to say. His ringing utterances, designed for the ears of the assembled company of veterans, were interspersed with sotto voce speeches of a mysterious character : —

" I ran him to ground at last, and when he found he couldn't get away, he — (Be still, can't you !) — gave up. But it was only by a subterfuge I got him here to-night. (No, I don't let you go so easy, old fellow !) And I know there's not a man here — (Oh, yes, I'll except you) — who will not rejoice to meet once more the most gallant, unselfish — (No, you don't choke me off now !) — modest hero that the Pennsylvania ——th ever numbered among her officers."

The colonel's voice rose to a shout with the last words.

" Quick, there ! Strike a light ! Head him off ! He's making for the door. Lock it ! He'll get away from us yet."

A dozen lights were struck. The chandeliers flashed up, a blaze of illumination. There was a cry, —

"Hurrah for the major!"

Everybody who was sitting down had jumped up and was pressing forward or trying to look over somebody else's head. Martin, eager as the rest, and curiously moved, he knew not why, mounted a chair, so that he out-topped the tallest veterans.

And what did he see?

Dr. John, caught in the very act of edging toward the door. Dr. John, looking like a detected criminal, as his old comrades laid hold of him and brought him back, reproaching him and cheering him in one breath. Dr. John, called upon for a speech, and starting out bravely, not to say defiantly, then faltering and breaking down, as old associations flooded his memory. Dr. John, protesting that he was no speech-maker, but rising to the occasion, nevertheless, and giving utterance to patriotic sentiments in a way that stirred the loyalty of the old veterans, and made the hall resound again with cheers. Dr. John, the hero of the evening, whose name and praises were on every tongue.

How small and mean Martin felt! What a goose and sneak and lunatic he had been! And when the doctor, his self-possession a little restored, though still protesting against the extravagant honors done him, catching sight of Martin, said pleasantly, "I think I see a young friend of mine over there," and called the lad to his side, how proud and unworthy Martin felt under the distinction.

But it was a great event for the young fellow, none the less, one to be treasured and remembered all his life, to be told over and over again to eager listeners at home, to be dwelt upon when the dark tragedy, already impending, descended upon the little colony beside The Brook.

CHAPTER XXXIX.

TROUBLE IN THE VALLEY.

The Grand Army disbanded, and the old soldiers went their separate ways, with many a cordial grasp of hands and many a dimmed eye.

Before Colonel Marshall and his nephew returned to their Eastern home, they made a long call at Home Ranch.

On this occasion Hope showed them a little collection of wild flowers she had pressed, that greatly interested them, and the colonel made inquiries about their growth and habits, which she was able to answer with intelligence.

Then they walked down into the rose garden, for a parting look at the "Agnes Clifford." After a short period of rest the plant was again putting forth a profusion of buds.

"How comes it, Miss Hope," asked the colonel, "that while you have so many roses, and a number of choice ones, I see that many of the standard kinds are not here, and you have none of the new roses that have been introduced during the last few years. Did you get tired of planting them?"

"Tired of roses? Oh, no, no, no!" cried Hope.

"But you felt that you had enough," suggested the colonel.

"No, Colonel Marshall," replied Hope, looking down, while her cheeks vied in color with the most brilliant of her crimson roses; "that wasn't it at all. Something happened that spoiled the pleasure for me. I used money that I ought not to have used. It was n't exactly dishonest, but it was wretchedly mean, and it made lots of trouble. I felt as if I could never buy another rose. Ned wanted to, but I would n't let him."

"Why, why!" exclaimed the colonel, hardly knowing whether to be most touched or amused by this confession, while Lieutenant Marshall did not take his eyes from the charming, downcast face.

"We will make that all right," pursued the colonel, breaking the awkward silence. "You don't need to pay out money for them. You have just been showing me something as good as gold with any Eastern florist."

"The — black rose?" asked Hope.

"No, my dear. That is a much more important matter, and I shall not make you an offer in regard to it until I am home and can consult with my head gardener. I mean your California wild-flowers, seeds and plants. I would n't ask for any better currency. Why can't you send them to me?"

"I should be very glad to do it," replied Hope warmly.

Then the colonel reverted to the subject of the black rose.

"Which would you like best, a specified sum outright, or a royalty on all the plants that are sold?"

"A 'royalty'?" repeated Hope inquiringly.

"Yes, a royalty. That means a certain percentage on all the sales, just as an author has a royalty on a book. Only, in this case, if you preferred the royalty, we should of course pay you a small sum outright, for there is no question as to the value of your rose, and there always is a very serious question as to whether a new book is worth the paper it is printed on."

"I think it would be very nice, and fair besides, to have the royalty," said Hope.

"Very well," said the colonel, looking pleased. "Now, Miss Hope, will you do me the kindness to accept a couple of small articles you will find very useful in your work among the flowers?"

Timid as a boy, yet with the stately courtesy of a gentleman of the old school, he drew a couple of small parcels from his pocket, and brought to light a pair of rubber gloves and some rose shears, which cut and held the rose at the same time, and which were destined to save Hope's tender hands from many a thorn.

The lieutenant lingered a little longer. Although he was a genuine West Point boy, who had passed unscathed through a dozen flirtations, this little maid, with her sweet face and untutored ways, had somehow won upon him as no other girl or woman had ever done.

"Miss Hope," he said in a low voice, "may I — shall I come back next year?"

The sixteen-year-old girl caught her breath with

a little gasp of surprise and terror. He was so handsome, so gentle-mannered, so amiable, such a thorough gentleman, every inch of him! She did not want to hurt him, and his blue eyes seemed wistfully pleading with her. Then the budding woman in her arose, and strengthened her to be true to herself and to him.

"Not on my account, Lieutenant Marshall," she said.

Why was it that at that very moment the memory of another scene bore in upon her, and she saw, in his place, a boy's tear-stained face, and heard the boyish cry : —

"Whatever I am — if I ever amount to anything, Hope, I owe it all to you."

Two weeks later they could scarcely believe that the Grand Army had come and gone, with all its train of exciting incidents. Dr. John (they could not call him by the name to which he was entitled, nor did he urge it) seemed just the same as ever. He had steadily resisted the importunities of the colonel to go back with him to his Eastern home, but it was noticeable that after the departure of the visitors he looked thin and worn. This was easily accounted for by the prevalence of a dangerous malarial fever throughout the valley. The constant demands upon him night and day, as well as the voluntary aid he rendered destitute sufferers, might well have taxed a stronger constitution than his.

Of course the McCrarys came down with it, just when the disease had abated a little and the doctor most needed rest.

Matters had somewhat changed at the mountain ranch, since Mike McCrary started out to prove himself a man. The house was in better repair and better furnished. A few flowering shrubs redeemed the untidy aspect of the dooryard. The children went to school, and Sam, at nineteen years of age, shamed into activity by Mike's example, had planted a considerable acreage in vines, to which he was giving indifferent care.

Nothing could make a change in the slack, incapable mother, however, and the children generally patterned after her.

One of the little girls, however, was cast in a different mould from the rest. She was a fair-haired child of thirteen, with sad blue eyes, wherein one seemed to read the story of her neglected childhood.

Little Mattie, as she was called, was a gentle, lovable girl, who under almost any other conditions would have been a general favorite. She was a diligent scholar, with pretty, lady-like ways, in notable contrast to the rough manners of the others. Hemmed in by every disadvantage, she had exerted all her slight strength to bring some order and decency to the dirty, unkempt house. Mike, striving all the while with a sense of humiliation as he contrasted his own home with the orderly households of the valley, where his industrious habits and jolly disposition made him a general favorite, was little Mattie's devoted champion, and secretly looked forward to some day installing her as housekeeper in a home of his own.

When the fever had run its race with the rest of the family, Mattie, the faithful and devoted nurse, fell sick, and Dr. John saw that it was to be a sharp struggle if he would save her.

Distracted at the danger that threatened his young sister, Mike McCrary left his work in the valley and came to her bedside, where he took up his quarters as a faithful and tireless watcher. Together the doctor and he fought for the child's life, and one night the crisis passed, and they knew they had won the fight.

With his finger on his lips, Dr. John arose and tiptoed out of the house. He felt strangely worn and tired, now that the sharp strain was over. He stretched out his arms, as if to relieve himself from the long tension, and looked up to the stars, glittering so brightly in the infinite reaches above him.

A footfall sounded on the turf, and Mike stood beside him, his haggard face dignified by its look of solemn thanksgiving.

"It's your work, Dr. John," he said. "You've saved her. There isn't anything in the world I wouldn't do for you. I'd lay down my life for you."

To Ned, Dr. John had become more of a mystery than ever he had been to Martin. Satisfied as he was that the doctor could never have done anything ignoble, the colonel's story, when he thought it over, was fragmentary and incomplete.

Why should a sick man flee from home and friends? In what had the doctor's sickness consisted? What had brought about his complete and miraculous recovery? and what did the doctor mean by his reference to the "abandoned claim," when first they came upon their homestead?

These were the questions that absorbed the young man's mind, and over which he might have continued to puzzle had not a weightier problem displaced them.

The occupants of Home Ranch became involved in a dispute which never could have occurred anywhere but in California.

A great corporation, which earned a princely revenue by supplying one of the largest cities in California with water, had long had its eye on The Brook, on account of its copious supply of clear water, drawn from living mountain streams. The supply of water in its reservoirs was becoming inadequate for the growing city's uses.

So the corporation went vigorously to work, buying up lands along the headwaters of The Brook, buying out some of the riparian owners along the line of the stream, confiscating other claims by means of a very favorable State law known as "A Bill defining certain Prescriptive Rights," and finally built a great dam to divert the waters of The Brook into its pipes.

The company began operations a couple of miles up the cañon, where the steep cliffs nearly approached each other, inclosing a considerable area, that only needed a heavy wall of stone across the entrance to complete a vast natural reservoir.

By the middle of August its work was completed, and just as the farmers came to the season of the year when water was most essential to them, the sparkling fluid that nature and the Almighty had decreed should refresh the valley coursed through it, imprisoned in an iron pipe, on its way to the city.

The people of the valley awoke to the fact that all of the conventions that had been called in their midst, the blatant speeches that had been made, had been an empty "bluff," a sham fight generaled by unscrupulous men who had sought thereby to get a better price from the Water Company. Several of these men sold their riparian privileges outright; others compromised for a liberal allowance of water daily. The poorer farmers, whose prosperity or ruin depended upon the security of their water rights, who had not the money to wage a long and unequal contest, and upon whom the loss of water for a single month entailed serious privation and loss, found the courts deaf to their appeals for immediate protection.

The Austins with difficulty watered their cattle from their spring, which had begun to show the effect of two successive dry seasons in a diminished flow of water, and saved sufficient for household purposes. The bed of The Brook was dry, and the hydraulic ram which they had put into the stream to water a tract of small fruits planted on the lower land was a useless encumbrance. Their figs were withering and dropping from the boughs; green raspberries shriveled and turned brown upon the bushes. Even Hope's roses began to look sickly, while garden vegetables parched in the sun without maturing. Their experience was typical of what was being undergone throughout the valley, and many were much worse off than they.

CHAPTER XL.

THE COURT OF LAST RESORT.

One still night early in September, as the boys were returning from their chores about the stable, Martin caught Ned's arm in excitement, pointing to the open stretch of road on the opposite side of The Brook.

The bridge and its approaches shone white in the moonlight, and the dead sycamore that stood guard on the further side of the water penciled a dark tracery of naked limbs against the starry sky. The ground beyond was dark with moving figures. Cattle? They watched for a moment before they could satisfy themselves. No, men, men on horseback, now crossing the bridge, which rang a muffled response to the clattering hoofs. Then the body seemed to pause, as if for brief deliberation. A moment later two mounted figures dashed up the lane.

The boys ran down to meet them. The horsemen drew rein.

"Mr. Willetts!" exclaimed Martin, wonderingly, as he recognized a steady young ranchman, who, with his wife and child, lived a couple of miles further down the stream.

"Boys," said the farmer, " we have business up the cañon to-night. Do you want to join us?"

No need of further explanation. Ned answered like a soldier to the roll-call:—

"I will come."

Then, seeing Martin's eager movement, he laid his hand on his brother's shoulder.

"Only one, Martin. If anything should happen, they must have you to depend upon," and he looked in the direction of the cottage.

"Make haste, Austin," said Willetts. "Bring an axe, hatchet, crowbar, — anything you have handy. No firearms, mind."

As the horsemen took their way up the cañon, any stranger who might have seen them would have been puzzled to make out their character and purpose. Surely, this was no gay cavalcade, bound on sport or pleasure, nor yet could it have been mistaken for a martial company, riding forth to open contest, where it expected to achieve honor and renown. No light jests passed. There was no laughter on the grim faces, no enthusiasm in the downcast eyes. It was more like a funeral party, for in his heart each loyal man rebelled against the position into which he had been forced, — that of an opponent to the peaceful administration of the laws of the State.

Yet they rode on and on, into the gloomy shadows of frowning cliffs, some with faces bent low, until their chins rested on their breasts, others with heads raised defiantly, nerved by the consciousness that whatever the result of their mission, they were the wronged; the great corporation the aggressor.

As they approached the third crossing of The Brook, a receding hillside let a flood of light into the narrow gorge where the company had erected its dam, revealing the dry and stony bed of the stream, with a fringe of perishing grasses along its margin. Tall alders, sycamores, and willows, which had established themselves long years before beside the stream, drooped low over its empty channel, and answered the night breeze with quivering sighs, as if mourning the inconstancy of the stream whose faithful wooers many of them had been for a century past.

A hundred yards above, a broad and glistening wall of stone crossed the gorge. Along this three armed men were pacing like sentinels on a rampart. The ripple of imprisoned waters could be heard above.

The sound maddened the ranchers. This was the precious fluid for want of which their stock was dying, their gardens and small fruit parching, their wells running dry.

"Halt! Who are you?"

It was one of the sentinels on the dam who challenged them.

Loud and clear came the reply: —

"We are seventy determined men from the valley. We want water."

"I am here to protect this dam. Don't you come nearer, or I'll fire."

The sentinel raised his rifle to his shoulder, and leveled it at the crowd.

One of the men on horseback pressed to the front, and as if in response to this movement the whole company surged forward.

There was a flash, a puff of smoke, and a loud report awoke the echoes of the cañon. The man who had first moved forward reeled in his saddle, and fell.

In the glamour of the moonlight no one seemed to recognize him. There were wild cries of, —

"He is killed!"

"Who is he?"

"No, he is all right. See! he is up again."

They had not dared close in around him, lest the horses, already terrified and prancing, should trample him down. Those near to him instinctively drew off, while one or two quickly dismounted and ran to his side, but before they could reach him he was on his feet, holding by the pommel of his saddle to steady himself.

"I only wanted a word with you, McCrary," he said, addressing the sentinel. "Listen to me now. These men are honest farmers, men you know and respect. Most of them settled in the valley, along the line of this stream, before the water company was incorporated. This water means life and subsistence to our people. Their crops are failing, — cattle dying. The stagnant pools along the bed of The Brook are breeding pestilence throughout the valley. . . . Be more than the faithful servant of a rich corporation. Be a man, and respect the rights of your fellowmen."

They could see that the man who had fired the rifle faltered in his purpose. He had lowered the gun, and seemed to be debating with himself as to what course he should pursue, while his two aids drew near and stood irresolute, awaiting his orders.

No one but those in his immediate vicinity had recognized the speaker. His voice, raised from the ordinary conversational tone, was deep and sonorous, qualities emphasized by the echoing crags above. In the moon's deceptive light, faces and forms, seen at a little distance, took on a foreign aspect.

He spoke again, and his hearers observed a huskiness and broken utterance, like one who battles against a growing physical weakness.

"Why, McCrary, are you so blind to all principles of right — that I must appeal — as man to man? Do you think — I — would join such a movement — if I did n't know — it was in the interests of justice? Don't let us have any more bloody work to-night. McCrary, you said once — you 'd do anything for me. Don't fire again — on unarmed men! Let me be the first — and the last — victim."

He was sinking in the arms of one who stood beside him. Blood was drenching his garments, and forming a pool upon the ground at his feet. At the last words Mike McCrary flung his rifle backward into the deep pool, and they heard a splash as it struck the water and sank.

He leaped down from the dam, and forced his way to the side of the injured man. None who heard him ever forgot his bitter cry: —

"O, my God! I've killed the doctor."

They made quick work of the dam after that.

Long before morning The Brook was rippling down the cañon, its old glad self, distributing its bounty throughout the valley, and cheering the face of all the country.

CHAPTER XLI.

THE DOCTOR'S STORY.

"Why, Mike, I understand. You thought it was your duty. You did n't know me."

Dr. John was lying on a litter the men had improvised for him. Even in his weakness and pain, he was mindful of others, and tried to comfort the poor fellow who hung over him in an agony of self-reproach, begging his forgiveness.

The wounded man gave directions to those about him with a self-command and hardihood that awed them; but his first thought was of the man who was accusing himself of having slain his best friend.

"Don't take on so, Mike. If any one had to go it is better it should have been me. I have — no one — to miss me."

"No one to miss him!" What a murmur of contradiction arose. Who could not be better spared? Who would be so sorely missed by all the country?

"It's nothing serious," insisted the doctor weakly. "I'll be all right in a week or two. Now take a place at the head, where the heaviest weight comes, Mike. You'll do penance enough over this long road. I'm no mean weight."

Dr. John did not speak again until the sorrowful procession rested a few moments near the bridge. Then he beckoned Ned to him, and spoke in an undertone : —

"Don't go home, Ned. Send word. I want you to stay by me — all the time. There is something — I must say to you — to-night."

The ball had passed through the doctor's side, coming out again at the back. Whether it was a mere flesh wound or had penetrated some vital organ was a matter for after demonstration.

Those who knew the doctor's radical precepts were not surprised when he directed that the wounds should be dressed with a simple wet compress; but they were amazed when he firmly declined their proposal to telegraph for another physician.

"I understand my case best," he insisted. "Ned is to be my chief nurse. McCrary will assist him. Now, friends, do not be offended if I thank you all, and ask you to leave me. I must prescribe rest and quiet for my patient."

When the door had closed behind the last one, and Mike McCrary had been dispatched into an adjoining room, Ned obeyed the doctor's gesture, and took a seat by his bedside.

Many minutes passed before Dr. John spoke, and as Ned waited his eye roved about the room, observing many little details of its arrangement.

It was a large chamber, running quite across the house, and a double window, on the side opposite the bed, looked out toward Home Ranch, and was embowered with sweet-scented honeysuckle in which the night twitter of birds was plainly audible. A small revolving bookcase and an easy-chair beside the casement attested that this was the doctor's study, as well as sleeping apartment. The room was furnished with the utmost simplicity. An ingrain rug was on the floor; a table, a few chairs, a writing-desk, and the ordinary chamber furniture completed the fittings of the room.

On the gray-tinted walls was a single picture, a painting of a woman, evidently copied from a miniature. The serious beauty of the high-bred face arrested Ned's attention. He had never seen a face that could compare with it, yet there was something in the expression of the mournful eyes that was peculiarly saddening.

He was relieved when the doctor at length moved, and he could withdraw his gaze from the fair face, with its sad, inquiring eyes.

Dr. John motioned toward a pitcher of ice water on a stand near by. Ned hastened to anticipate his want.

"Had n't you better wait, sir, — until to-morrow, perhaps? You are so weak. It might hurt you to talk now. After a good night's rest" —

"This is nothing," exclaimed Dr. John. "Loss of blood, nothing more. But I'm not in the best bodily condition, Ned, and this is going to bring back an old trouble. Ned, I'm going to ask of you as great a service as one man ever asked of another."

Ned did not speak in reply, but his look held a pledge that the doctor understood.

"Ned, Marshall didn't tell the whole truth — that night at the camp-fire. He glossed over facts. I came out of the army suffering with a painful neuralgic trouble, the result of a gunshot wound. I took opium to ease the pain. When I got the better of the disease I was a slave to the drug.

"I'm not able to go into details now. I had a wife, and afterwards a little daughter was born. They were dearer to me than my own soul; but a man who once becomes enslaved by that damnable habit would pledge his soul for a single grain of the drug. I started in with a tolerably good practice, but half the time I was unfit to attend to my patients. My child fell sick. We thought she could not get well. I did what I could for her, but instead of trying to comfort my poor wife I took larger and larger doses. It helped me not to care. I kept sinking lower and lower. My credit was gone. I was mad for the drug. Ned, I did a dastardly thing. I robbed the little savings bank of our dying child, and she, — my wife, — saw me."

The doctor ceased speaking, and pointed to the glass of water. Ned held it to his lips, and after a pause Dr. John resumed his story.

"She did not say a word, but she pointed to the door. I went out into the night, an abased, God-forsaken creature. . . . I slept on the ground under a tree in the public park that night. I didn't dare go back; I thought the child was dead; but then and there I made a desperate resolve to free myself from that accursed habit or die in the attempt. I started out into the country. . . . I can't tell you the horrors I went through. I can't bear to recall them to this day. I could neither eat nor sleep, but I walked — walked — walked ; scores upon scores of miles, always avoiding towns, stopping at farm-houses, working for my meals when I was able to swallow anything ; now and then putting in a week or so working in the field. It was seed-time when I started out, and it was harvest-time when I was through. The return to a simple, healthful life, the exercise of disused muscles, the absence of temptation and opportunity, had effected a cure. . . . But I could n't go back. . . . Ned, I 'm going to pass through a season of terrible pain. I 'm afraid of myself. There 's a bottle of arsenic and a bottle of morphine, side by side, on the shelf in my cabinet in the next room."

"I 'll go and empty out the morphine, burn it up, — bury it," said Ned, anticipating the request the doctor was about to make.

The doctor's head moved nervously on the pillow ; a contemptuous expression flitted over his face.

"The principle on which they are trying to run three fourths of the reformatory institutions in the country," he said dryly. "Preserving men from temptation by shutting off temptation from them. As if any lasting good could ever be accomplished without strengthening a man's moral nature ! No, Ned. Let the bottles stand there ; only, if worst comes to worst, if I am so weak as to beg for the opiate, promise me you'll give me the quicker poison first."

The doctor was so earnest in his appeal that Ned gave the singular pledge without a second's thought.

"Now you know — why I don't want — any woman around. You understand — why I don't — want — another doctor, — why I would rather . . . depend on . . . you and Mike."

The doctor's short and labored breath showed that his long effort in speaking was telling on him. Ned arranged the lights in the room so as to throw the bed into the shadow, and was soon rejoiced to see his patient pass into a deep slumber.

CHAPTER XLII.

THE LAST BATTLE.

THE hero of many battles had one more to fight, and it was a battle unto the death.

Ned kept a vigilant watch over the sick-bed that first night, not even lying down when Mike insisted upon relieving him.

Their patient slept so heavily that both watchers, unable to discriminate between the sleep of health and the sleep of exhaustion, were greatly rejoiced, and looked confidently forward to a marked improvement the next day ; but towards dawn the sick man began to show symptoms of restlessness and fever, and he awoke in violent pain.

Day after day went by with little change in the doctor's condition. He gave directions for his own treatment, which were scrupulously obeyed by his faithful nurses.

In the intervals of respite from pain, he would lie calmly looking out of the open window embowered with honeysuckles, his thoughts far away. Sometimes his eyes were fixed upon the portrait, and at such times there came into them a look of sorrow and of longing pitiful to see.

Rarely he aroused himself for a few words of

conversation. On one occasion when he and Ned were alone, he spoke to the boy in a weak and failing voice: —

"If I should get pretty low, Ned, . . . so far gone that there seems to be no other hope, I suppose Dr. Thompson had better be called in. But don't be in a hurry. This is going to be a matter of weeks, not days."

"Sha'n't we send for him now?" asked poor Ned, who would willingly have had some more mature judgment upon which to lean.

"No. Just at the last, for decency's sake," replied Dr. John. "I don't want to go out of the world . . . and leave . . . a reputation for pig-headed obstinacy . . . behind me. But mind, no opiates, even if he prescribes them."

"I don't believe you would take them if he gave them to you. You underrate your own moral courage, Dr. John," said Ned earnestly.

"You don't know, Ned, you don't know," said the doctor weakly. "Only a physician knows what miserable, cowardly, tyrannic forces . . . these bodies of ours are; how they buffet, and torment, and cow . . . the soul. Stronger men than I have given up, — stronger men than I."

He lay with his eyes closed.

"I don't believe a human body ever held a stronger soul," cried Ned in a burst of enthusiasm.

The doctor opened his eyes once more, turning upon Ned a glance of gratitude, simple and unfeigned as a child's. Possibly the young fellow's faith helped to strengthen him for the struggle before him, so dependent are we all upon the sympathy and confidence of our fellow-beings.

Thus he glided into the heat of the awful conflict that disease was about to wage with the spirit for the possession of its abused and worn-out tenement.

In all this time the old weakness, whose return he had so dreaded, never once overcame him. Sometimes when the pain and fever were at their height, when it seemed as if exhausted nature must cry aloud for some relief from the agony that racked the enfeebled frame, the sufferer would turn to Ned with a flitting smile that seemed to say, "Still holding out!"

At such times Ned always answered with a look of undiminished courage.

After all, it was Ned whose courage failed, and not the doctor.

One day there came upon the sufferer a paroxysm of pain such as Ned had never witnessed before, but such as he was destined to witness many times during the weeks to come, each one drawing the sick man nearer to the Valley of the Shadow of Death, which he was about to enter.

Ned forgot his promise, forgot everything save that before him was lying his best friend, suffering as it seemed no mortal could long suffer and live, while near at hand was a remedy that would silence the pain and bring him relief.

He rushed into the next room, threw open the doors of the cabinet, seized the bottle, and returned to the bedside of Dr. John with it in his hand.

If he had known the proper dose he would have measured it out and administered it; not having the faintest idea of the proper quantity, he could only hold it out to Dr. John and beg him to take it.

An indescribable look came into the sick man's face; a look of fearful longing mingled with terror shone in his eyes as they fell on the drug. Then he raised his clenched fist and trembling smote the bottle from the young man's hand.

"Why, Ned!" he gasped, fixing a reproachful gaze upon him.

It was the most humiliating moment of the young fellow's life. Long years after he remembered the doctor's look and heard the reproachful words. Without pausing to think, he caught up the bottle and flung it into the grate, where a low fire had been kindled to remove the morning's chill. There was a crash of glass, and then the greedy flames licked up the white powder.

A moment's respite from the deathly pain that racked him would have been a priceless boon to the sick man; yet he never slept save in fitful dozes from which he awoke moaning in anguish. He preserved consciousness until the morning of the twenty-fourth day, when, a little past midnight, a deadly torpor crept over mind and body. His muscles, hitherto strained with unnatural tension, relaxed. His limbs, cramped with pain, grew limp and motionless. His clenched hands fell weakly by his side or idly plucked the counterpane.

No need of opiates now. The delicate nerves,

chords of physical sensation, swept again and again by the merciless throes of pain, were like the worn-out strings of some frail musical instrument, and no longer responded to the touch.

Ned, who had never once relaxed his vigils over the sick man, snatching sleep like a young watch-dog, at the bedside, found that the clear intellect had at last become clouded. A slow lethargy was stealing over mind as well as body. His frantic demands for some sign that the doctor still recognized him brought only a stammering, wandering response.

The boy's task was ended. More skill than he possessed was needed, if, indeed, human aid could longer avail.

Mike was waiting below. It had become apparent, at an early stage of the doctor's illness, that the poor fellow was not a fit attendant for the sick man. His constant self-reproaches, his awkward and noisy movements, disturbed the sensitive patient, and the unfortunate fellow voluntarily abdicated his place as nurse, and constituted himself an humble helper and man of all work, performing every menial task, bringing lights, fuel, water; preparing bandages, going on errands, and answering numberless calls from anxious inquirers.

Ned found him waiting in the little office below, seated on the edge of one of the stuffed leather chairs, a look of deep anxiety on his face.

Ned could not speak. They stared at each other, trying to find words for what they felt, and courage to pronounce them.

" Is it — is it that?" blundered Mike at last.

"Yes, Mike. I am afraid."

Mike crumpled his hat — it was his Sunday best — between his hands, jamming it into a shapeless lump, as if in this act he might find relief for his over-charged heart.

"Any man but him! If it had been any man but him!" he finally broke out. "What'll all the valley do without him? Who is there to take his place?"

This brought to Ned the memory of a forgotten injunction.

"That reminds me, Mike," he said hastily, "I was to send for old Dr. Thompson in case this — in case the worst came to pass. I promised him to do so. Will you carry word now?"

"I'll go right off," cried Mike, starting up, eager to do something, to be of use to the friend who had already passed beyond knowledge of all human effort. During all the doctor's illness, the possible consequences to himself never occurred to the unhappy fellow. The law held no such terror for him as the possibility of the doctor's death by his hand.

"I'll run there afoot as fast as any man can ride," he cried, darting through the door.

It may well be imagined that when the news of the doctor's injury was conveyed to Home Ranch, it had occasioned the greatest distress and anxiety there. Hope had hastily packed in a valise such articles as she thought Ned would need, and carried it to him herself.

As she handed it to him, she gave him four folded silk handkerchiefs, red, blue, black, and white, presents from Ah Wing, the doctor's Chinese servant, on as many successive China New Years.

"Ned," she said, "we shall all want to know how the doctor is getting along, oftener than we can send or come. We want to know all the time. Take these handkerchiefs, and keep one of them hanging out of the upper window that looks towards The Brook, — the blue one if he is worse, the white one if he is better, the red one if he will surely, surely get well, and — oh, Ned! — the black one, if there is no more hope."

Ned promised to remember the signals, and day after day the blue handkerchief had fluttered from the window, conveying its discouraging tidings to the three watchers across The Brook. This morning, before dawn, Ned went to the place where he had laid the handkerchiefs, and, untying the blue one, hung the dark messenger of sorrow in its stead.

Time dragged wearily by. He did not know till long after that Mike had a chase of ten miles across the country before he found the old physician, whose practice had been materially increased during Dr. John's illness.

In the sick-room, where the shades were kept raised all day to let in the fresh air and sunshine in obedience to the doctor's principles, the cheery aspect of the room, as the morning light crept in, seemed to breathe of hope and new life rather than of death and decay. The honeysuckle at the window shed its fragrance throughout the room. Occasionally its foliage rustled musically as it answered the touch of a vagrant breeze. Honeybees buzzed past, laden with spoils from the hearts of the brilliant blossoms on the lawn, and once a tiny humming-bird, a marvel of glittering bronze, with a crimson collar and breast, darted into the room and poised motionless in mid-air, its outspread wings twinkling like the rays of some magnificent jewel, then darted out again as swiftly, as if it could not abide the sight the room contained.

The white hands no longer roved restlessly over the counterpane, but lay still and almost pulseless on the sick man's breast. His face was wan and colorless, and his features sharpened by his long and wasting illness. His breath came in long, fluttering gasps, and his eyes were glazed and sightless.

Even as Ned watched him he saw a look of perfect peace, the look that the dying wear, spread over the doctor's face. Indeed, he looked so like death that the solitary young watcher bent over him in an agony of grief and pain, to make sure that the breath of life still faintly came and went between the parted lips.

To Ned, awed and appalled by the nearness of a presence strange to him, all the sights and sounds of the outside world faded into dim reality. Nothing was real or tangible but the sick man, stretched out on the bed before him, fast progressing beyond the reach of human power, and the pictured face on the wall, which seemed to look down, a sentient, breathing being.

The welcome sound of carriage wheels broke upon the silence. Ned crossed the room and looked out of a window, only to be disappointed.

It was not the old doctor's phaeton, but a public conveyance from the station. Two ladies had alighted, and were walking swiftly towards the house. They were some visitors who had come to inquire after the doctor, he thought. Yet he stepped into the hall and looked down.

They were already in the doorway, speaking with Wing. Ned had only time to observe that they were clad in dark gray ulsters and had a look as if they had come on a long journey. At the sound of steps above, one of them lifted her face.

Ned clung to the balustrade, his head in a whirl. In the hall's dim light he saw a pale, oval face with pathetic dark eyes. Years of sorrow had dimmed the radiance of youth, but had no power to quench the imperishable beauty of the face.

It was the original of the portrait.

"Where is he? Take me to him."

She was climbing the stairs, and there was mingled entreaty and command in her voice.

Ned turned silently back to the doctor's room, past the landing, on through the narrow passageway, to the sunshiny room where a noble life was nearing its close.

She gave one low cry as she saw the still, white

face. Then she sped noiselessly to the bedside and bent over the dying man.

"Oh, my husband! Speak to me. Look at me."

Not so much as the flicker of an eyelid answered her passionate call.

"My darling! Tell me that you hear me. I have come to you. Make some sign, one word to tell me that you know me."

Hewn stone could not have been more motionless, iron more irresponsive, than the inanimate figure.

Then Ned and the younger lady, standing together near the door, not daring to move lest they should startle the anguish-stricken woman, became witnesses of a terrible and heart-breaking scene.

Despairingly she chafed the hands of the dying man, placing her lips to them again and again. She stroked the thick brown hair back from the forehead, where the death-damp was gathering. She pressed her cheek against his, with a wife's supreme love, but tenderly as a mother caresses her child. And all the while she poured into the deaf ears broken protestations of the pent-up affection and grief of years.

"Oh, my darling! My poor boy! Hear me. Awake and listen to me, if only for a moment. I loved you then — I love you now — more than life. Even then, — that cruel night when I drove you away, — you, my poor, unfortunate husband! — when I should only have been more tender and pitiful. Hear me, dear! I was sick — sick, when the colonel told me. I came as soon as I could travel. I loved you always, my brave, noble, unselfish hero. Come back — come back to me! that I may prove it, and make up to you for the long, lonely, terrible years we have spent apart. My God, help me! Give him back. Tell him how I have waited and prayed and looked for him. Eighteen years! And then to find him only for this. Oh, my God!"

She did not cease even when a rattling vehicle came noisily up the road, and the sound of a gruff voice below told that the old physician had at last arrived.

Ned and the young lady were crying helplessly by the door when Dr. Thompson entered. They tried to keep him back a little, and to give the other lady warning of his approach, but there was no need. At the sound of the opening door she had arisen, controlling herself by a strong effort. Bowing with dignified recognition of the physician's entrance, she awaited his verdict with sad and hopeless eyes.

Dr. Thompson was a thin, cadaverous old gentleman, with a sombre countenance, suggestive of undertakers and funerals. He walked into the room with a pompous air. There had never been much sympathy between him and Dr. John. Too many patients whom the old doctor had given over to die had been saved by the younger man, and were living witnesses to the whole community of his skill — or shall we say his common sense?

Dr. Thompson was an old fogy, it is true, but even old fogies do not like to be superseded by younger men with better schooling and more progressive ideas. Therefore it was with a pardonable feeling of triumph that the old doctor had answered the call to his younger colleague's bedside. He had taken pains to inform everybody he met that Dr. John was worse and had sent for him.

It was something to have his rival prostrate and helpless, and obliged at last to appeal to his professional skill.

He drew back with a start at the bedside. What was this?

Instead of the petulant sufferer he had expected to see, chafing under his enforced confinement, here was a man already marked with death, silently passing into the great unknown; one to whom earthly rivalries and differences were no longer a matter of moment.

"How long has he been so?"

The old physician was startled out of his customary composure; he put the question to Ned.

"Since four o'clock this morning, sir. I sent immediately for you."

Dr. Thompson stooped and placed his ear to Dr. John's chest, laying his finger on his pulse. Then he drew from his pocket a slender rubber case, and took from it a small glass tube, which he slipped within the parted lips.

This thermometer was Dr. Thompson's one concession to modern science. He used it on all occasions, and, it was said, even diagnosed disease by means of it. This time he drew it out and looked at it, and then around at the others, with an air of owlish importance.

"Will he live?" asked Ned, and the lady's eyes repeated the question.

Now Dr. Thompson knew enough of the signs of approaching dissolution to be sure there was no mortal hope for Dr. John. But he had his own professional dignity to maintain, and knew that it would never answer to come so many miles to declare his inability to be of use.

"H'm!" he said, straightening himself and fastening his thumbs in the buttonholes of his coat. "H'm! A bad case, a serious case, madam. If I had been called sooner, — but, ahem, as I was not"—

They awaited his next words in breathless silence.

"There is just one thing that may possibly save him," said the old doctor, in a deep voice. "He must have an emulsion!"

The old physician's emulsions were the terror of every household in the valley. Dr. John had once been known to say that more people had died from Dr. Thompson's emulsions than he had ever saved. Dr. Thompson had heard of this speech, and there had been bad blood between the two physicians ever since.

Now, whether they are right or wrong, the people of the valley always will have it that Dr. John's professional spirit was stronger than death itself. Be that as it may, what patient care and tender nursing had failed to effect, what love itself had been powerless to accomplish, was brought about by this projected outrage upon his own code of practice.

For the sick man's hand, which an instant before had lain white and nerveless upon his breast, trembled, moved, then lifted, with a slight repellant gesture, wavered, and fell back.

The little group was startled. Even the old doctor, accustomed as he was to dying men, was shocked at this unexpected manifestation; but he repeated his decision, in an oracular tone: —

"He must have an emulsion."

This time the pallid lips quivered, the head moved slightly, and a faint whisper broke the silence : —

"I'll — die — first."

Be it dead or dying man who spoke, the assertion was a direct challenge of the old gentleman's medical skill. He took it up instantly, with a snort of indignation.

"You'll die without it, sir."

Dr. John was so weak that he could not raise his head from the pillow, but his eyes, wide open now, blazed with indignant fire. A world of stern resolve made itself felt in his halting utterance : —

"I'll — get — well — without — it, sir."

"Very well, sir. A fine example of professional courtesy, sir. I bid you good-day, sir."

A smile, sudden and fleeting, played about the lips of Dr. John. Then his whole face lighted with a look of exalted happiness, such as Ned had never seen there before. He stretched out his hand.

"Mary! My wife!"

She fell on her knees beside him without a word or cry. Great joy, like great sorrow, is often speechless. Husband and wife, reunited after so many years of separation, could find no words in which to express the emotions of their overflowing hearts.

"Father, have you no word for me?"

The young girl had stolen up to the bed. The memory of her fatherless childhood, the love and longing for the dear father who had left her in her babyhood, and who had never come back, quivered in her sweet voice. The doctor looked at her as one who dares not believe the hope that springs in the heart. As he gazed upon her fair young face, doubt slowly retreated and hope blossomed into a glad certainty. With a low exclamation he reached out his wasted hand, and the girl bent over it, bathing it with her tears.

CHAPTER XLIII.

THE MIRACLE A BLUNDER WROUGHT.

NED fled to the hall outside. The doctor was better. The doctor would get well. The doctor's wife and daughter had come to him!

All the weariness and despondency of the past few weeks fell from him as if by magic! He saw Mike McClary coming, and shouted the glad news to him, then ran off, hatless, towards the bridge, to carry his happy tidings to the anxious watchers at Home Ranch, little guessing the miracle that had been wrought there by his own blunder.

He had crossed the bridge, and was just turning into the garden path, when he saw Hope, bareheaded, and with her long work-apron tied about her waist, running toward him.

"Oh, Ned! Father — father — father!" she cried, and caught him by the lapels of his coat, sobbing as if her heart would break.

An awful fear laid hold upon Ned, rebuking his glad sense of thanksgiving at Dr. John's convalescence.

"Dead?" he exclaimed in a tragical voice, while something rose in his throat and almost strangled him.

"Come! Come quick!" she cried excitedly, catching his hand and hurrying him toward the house.

Not dead, thank Heaven! but living. Upon the threshold of a new life, with a renewed lease of health and strength. Standing on the porch, unassisted, but feeble and uncertain as a babe when it first begins to totter through the world. On his feet for the first time in five years, looking at Ned with the old cheerful smile and a proud flush on his face.

"And he can walk, too," cried Hope. "It was when you hung out the signal. We had all been watching for it since daybreak. We could hardly coax him to eat his breakfast, and when he was through we wheeled him to the window and left him there. He thought he saw something bright, but the branches of the pepper-trees hung between. And he was sure it was the red handkerchief, and he could n't wait for us to come to make certain."

"The red handkerchief!" repeated Ned in surprise.

"Yes, the red handkerchief, of course. Oh, how glad we all were! See it waving now."

And there, true enough, was the red handkerchief waving in the breeze, flapping against the perfumed branches of the honeysuckle, scaring the humming-birds from their field of sweets.

Ned knew then that a miracle had been wrought. In the dim light of early dawn he had mistaken the red for the black, and it had restored his father.

"And he walks as well as ever," rejoiced Hope. "But father, dear," she remonstrated, "you must not stand so long. You are not strong enough. He has been standing there ever since, Ned. We can't get him to sit down."

"Oh, children!" began Mr. Austin; and then he stopped and choked back something, ruling himself as a strong man must, when he feels himself in danger of giving away. "You don't know what it is to have the use of my body again. It's been a terrible trial, — to feel that I was no good in the world, — to know I was only a burden to you!"

"A burden!" repeated Hope indignantly, and the boys echoed the cry.

"Well, I suppose I must give up now," said the father, for his legs were weak, and he felt them failing beneath him. "Here, Ned, your shoulder, if you please."

Resting lightly on Ned's arm, he got back into the invalid chair.

"I warn you it won't be for long," he said, as he settled back into its comfortable depths. "I'm going to take a hand in the fruit picking next season, and there's a patch of ground back of the house — that vegetable garden of yours — that you don't half take care of. I've been aching to hoe it for a year."

CHAPTER XLIV.

PROVING UP.

Several weeks later a pleasant little party assembled under the shade of the pepper-trees in the dooryard of Home Ranch. All of the family were there, the boys taking a little respite from their cares, while Hope, in her plain frock of blue cambric, with bands of white at the neck and wrists, had put aside her sewing out of honor to her visitors.

The burden of housework had lately been lifted from her young shoulders, so happily and unexpectedly that it seemed like a chapter from some domestic Arabian Nights, for Biddy McGinnis one day presented herself, decently clad in widow's weeds. The last of her sons had deserted her to marry a young schoolgirl, and her worthless little husband had at length fallen a victim to the mania for strong drink that had always possessed him. Biddy herself, trying hard to disguise her sensation of relief with a decent mantle of sorrow, announced her intention of spending the rest of her days at Home Ranch and caring for the family as if they were her own. Hope was unceremoniously turned out of the kitchen, and bidden to stay in the parlor where she belonged, while all of them were "mothered" and looked after in the most tyrannical and affectionate fashion.

The doctor was in the invalid chair this time, his face still thin and colorless from the effects of his illness, but wearing a look of happiness that gladdened all their hearts. Mr. Austin, a little arrogant in the consciousness of his new-found health, as long-time invalids are wont to be, waited upon him in an ostentatious manner that amused the young people and brought a gleam of fun to the doctor's eyes.

Mrs. Sherwood was at the doctor's side, and their daughter, Bessie, sat at his feet, on the upper step of the little porch, in the shadow of the vines, where she could watch the others and escape observation herself.

Hope had been a little afraid of this accomplished and talented girl. Bessie Sherwood had been accustomed to the best society all her life. She had received a thorough education in all that it befits a young lady to know. She had been under the constant tutelage of a mother who was not only a true lady, but a wise and sensible woman. In her own little circle she had been somewhat noted for her gifts of mind and graces of person: she had even written for the newspapers, and written very well; yet she was shyer still of the child-woman who presided over Home Ranch than ever Hope could have been of her.

"She embarrasses me, with her odd, direct ways

and her simple dignity," Bessie explained to her parents. "It does n't matter if she does wear plain gowns; she has the air of an archduchess. Where did she learn such manners, papa dear?"

"From the hills and fields and stream. Dame Nature is a noble teacher. Hope Austin has had no other, my little girl," replied the doctor fondly.

There was something indescribably touching in the renewed intercourse between father and daughter. Each seemed to be perpetually trying to go back to the precious years they had lost, the years of dearest companionship between parent and child. The girl clung to the pet titles that had been a memory of her babyhood. The father refused to acknowledge her young ladyhood, or to accept her as anything more or less than an expanded image of the little child he had left.

Had the young people at Home Ranch been less generous-hearted or more selfish in their attachment to him, they might have resented the new claim that had seized upon the doctor, — their Dr. John, — who had hitherto seemed to belong wholly to them. As it was, they rejoiced that the shadows were forevermore banished from his home.

"Now, Ned, you have a report from Washington, I hear. What do the authorities say at last?" asked the doctor.

"I don't think you will want to hear it all," said Ned, drawing a cumbrous document from his breast pocket. "It is a full report of the case: opinions from this high authority and references to that; recommendations of one official, concurrences of others, and dissenting judgments of others. The sum and substance of it all is that our application is denied, and we now have to wait three years longer, to perfect the contingent entry made in the name of our father " —

" Who stands here a living testimonial to the logic of their decision," interrupted the doctor, smiling upon his whilom nurse.

" But it took them a good many years to make up their minds," criticised Martin.

" Never mind. We can afford to wait," said Ned cheerfully. " This season has put us well ahead. We can make the house a little more comfortable now, and add a room or two. We have been figuring it out, Martin and I, and I think that next year we can count upon a clear income of a couple of thousand dollars."

" And an increase every year, as the trees and vines get older, and new ones are put in, to say nothing of what we may make extra by putting the hill land into olives," added Martin.

" Not too fast, my boy ! " warned the doctor. " Phylloxera may lay hold of the vines, hot northers strike the fruit, new pests develop. Recollect, too, that the State is settling up fast, and every year's increased production forces the market down. The day for fancy prices is fast going by. Fruit raising will soon be on the same basis as any other legitimate business, commanding only a fair return for the labor expended, and a reasonable interest on the money invested."

"At any rate, we are sure of a comfortable home and an independent living. I count that most," said Hope.

"One of these days, when you have secured the title to your land," resumed the doctor, with a kind look at Hope, but trying hard to keep the conversation down to a business basis, "if you choose to cut up the ranch, you might sell off a portion at a good figure. Keep on cultivating, and planting trees and vines. Values are jumping everywhere around us. In a few years people will begin to appreciate the hill lands. I predict that within two years you can command a couple of hundred dollars an acre for any you choose to sell, providing only that it is tillable."

A couple of hundred dollars an acre! The young people had always thought of their home as a fixed possession, something that could not be bartered and sold. But it was true that nearly a hundred acres might be spared, and their cares greatly lightened thereby, while the essential portion of the ranch would still remain intact. They made a hasty calculation.

"Why, we should be rich!" exclaimed Martin.

"But richer still in health, happiness, and content," said the doctor's wife softly.

"I would n't sell an acre, if it were mine," said Bessie Sherwood, with animation, and she smiled as she met Ned's eyes fixed upon her with a look of frank approval.

There never could be any restraint or embarrassment between these two. Together they had watched a human soul, dear to them both, come back from the borderland of that mysterious region we call Death. They felt as if they had known each other all their lives.

"I don't believe I could possibly feel any richer than I do now. I feel like a millionaire twice over," said Hope quaintly, drawing a letter from her pocket. "This came last night. It is from Colonel Marshall."

She read the letter aloud: —

PHILADELPHIA, *November* —, 188–.

MY DEAR MISS HOPE, — After due consultation with my head gardener, who is already quite an enthusiast over our "black rose," we have determined to offer you five hundred dollars in cash for the exclusive control of the "Agnes Clifford," and a royalty of twenty per cent on all our sales of the rose. I am so sure that you have sufficient confidence in me to accept my offer that I take the liberty to inclose my check for the first-named amount. I should like to have the young plants you have rooted shipped to me at once, that I may get them safely housed for their winter growth.

Please convey my warmest regards to Dr. Sherwood, as well as his estimable wife, whom I have known from her childhood; also to their charming daughter, whose companionship I know you will prize.

Present my respects to your father and your

brothers, and accept for yourself the assurance of an old soldier's stoutest devotion.

Your obedient servant,
ROBERT L. MARSHALL.

" And what are you going to do with your check, Hope? Bank it, or invest in a gold mine, or buy a piano, books, pictures, new clothes, jewelry, — what?" quizzed the doctor.

" A buggy," replied Hope seriously. " The nicest, most comfortable that can be found, so that father can drive about every day. Oh, he thinks he is as strong as any one, but he isn't, doctor, and he needs to be watched and scolded like a child."

Brightly and cheerily as Hope had spoken, Bessie Sherwood, who had been watching her narrowly, saw a troubled shadow on her sweet young face.

There was one clause in Colonel Marshall's letter that Hope had suppressed, but that she could not put from her mind. It weighed upon her perpetually, like a prophecy of coming trouble.

Tucked away in a little postscript, at the end of the page, there had been a few words addressed to her alone : —

"My nephew insists on repeating his visit to California this coming year. He is a noble fellow. Be good to him, my dear."

That was what made the pain. If he were less worthy, it would not be so hard. But to inflict such pain upon him, to possibly be the means of clouding his whole life!

The tender-hearted girl was deeply distressed, and moved by sorrowful forebodings.

Suddenly Bessie Sherwood, still absently watching Hope's face, saw it flush with delight, and followed the direction of her eyes.

Tom Bateman was coming up the path.

Yet Tom had less to say to Hope than to any of the rest. When he had exchanged greetings with them all, he addressed himself to Ned.

"What news from Washington? Is your claim established?"

"It will be three years more before we can 'prove up,'" was the reply.

"You are lucky to get through so soon, Ned. There seems to be no limit to the time an ordinary man requires to 'prove up'—to his own satisfaction, to say nothing of—anybody else," observed Tom seriously, and his eyes for an instant sought Hope's, which were at once shyly averted, while his mute question remained unanswered.

"It isn't a question of years. It is a question of a lifetime, Tom," said the doctor earnestly; but the quick touch of his wife's hand upon his own, and her look of loving confidence, seemed to challenge his assertion.

www.ingramcontent.com/pod-product-compliance
Lightning Source LLC
Chambersburg PA
CBHW021159230426
43667CB00006B/467